Web Design on a Shoestring

WITHDRAWN

Carrie Bickner

Contents at a Glance

Web Design on a Shoestring

Copyright © 2004 by New Riders Publishing

International Standard Book Number: 0-7357-1328-6

Library of Congress Catalog Card Number: 2002110727

Printed in the United States of America

First edition: September 2003

08 07 06 05 04 03   7 6 5 4 3 2 1

Interpretation of the printing code: The rightmost double-digit number is the year of the book's printing; the rightmost single-digit number is the number of the book's printing. For example, the printing code 03-1 shows that the first printing of the book occurred in 2003.

Trademarks

Warning and Disclaimer

Associate Publisher
Stephanie Wall

Production Manager
Gina Kanouse

Acquisitions Editor
Michael Nolan

Senior Development Editor
Jennifer Eberhardt

Senior Project Editor
Sarah Kearns

Copy Editor
Krista Hansing

Indexer
Lisa Stumpf

Proofreader
Lori Lyons

Composition
Wil Cruz
Amy Hassos

Manufacturing Coordinator
Dan Uhrig

Cover and Interior Designer
Alan Clements

Marketing
Scott Cowlin
Tammy Detrich
Hannah Onstad Latham

Publicity Manager
Susan Nixon

 New Riders

800 East 96th Street
3rd Floor
Indianapolis, Indiana 46240

An Imprint of Pearson Education

BOSTON • INDIANAPOLIS • LONDON • MUNICH • NEW YORK • SAN FRANCISCO

This book is dedicated to my parents, for kicking cancer's ass twice in one year.
To my sister, for Sundays at eleven.
And above all, to my love, Jeffrey.

Table of Contents

About the Author

Photo by Edria Collins

Carrie Bickner is the Assistant Director for Digital Information and System Design at The New York Public Library. Bickner writes for *A List Apart*, *Library Journal*, and *Technology Electronic Reviews*, as well as for her personal site, `roguelibrarian.com`. She is the co-author of The NYPL Online Style Guide, a manual for transitioning to CSS and XHTML. She is a popular speaker at conferences such as Web Design World and The Public Library Association annual meeting, as well as SXSW.

She has worked on projects small and large, managing and producing $3,000 sites, $3 million sites, and everything in between. Bickner's current work includes NYPL Digital Gallery, a digital library of more than 100,000 images from the collections of The New York Public Library, and *The African-American Migration Experience*, an online multimedia encyclopedia documenting 13 phases of the African Diaspora, beginning with the international slave trade.

Carrie lives in New York City. When she has a free moment, she likes dabbling in amateur photography, watching classic movies, and pounding the endless blocks of Manhattan.

About the Technical Reviewers

These reviewers contributed their considerable hands-on expertise to the entire development process for *Web Design on a Shoestring*. As the book was being written, these dedicated professionals reviewed all the material for technical content, organization, and flow. Their feedback was critical to ensuring that *Web Design on a Shoestring* fits our reader's need for the highest-quality technical information.

Chad Brandt

Chad Brandt is the Web Services Manager at Best Software's Small Business Division in Scottsdale, Arizona. A cross-breed web designer/developer with an equal appreciation for quality programming and exceptional design, Chad is passionate about usability, contingency design, and most recently, web standards. In addition to his career at Best Software, Chad spends time building compelling, user-friendly web sites and web applications through his freelance business, Active Internet Solutions (www.activei.com).

Chad founded Active Internet Solutions (activei) in 1998 to offer cost-effective, enterprise-level web solutions to businesses of all size, type, and industry. "Web design on a shoestring" is a familiar concept to Chad, based on the number of budget-friendly web architecture/design services he provides for businesses with little to no budgets at all.

Allison Cecil

Whether it was forging straight-A report cards or drawing lemonade-stand signs, design was a part of Allison's life from an early age. Although she briefly pursued art in college, she got tired of wearing black and left her artiste aspirations behind. Upon moving to New York five years ago, black once again became her uniform and her interest in design was piqued. So she proceeded to enroll in Parsons School of Design where she learned that design is not just about pretty pictures.

After a three-year stint with magazine and web design guru Roger Black, Allison struck out on her own. Her clients present her with challenging projects in both web and print. These clients have included New Riders Publishing, Market News International, Watson Adventures, J. Crew, and *The National Enquirer*.

Allison's hobbies include reading dead writers, riding her pony around Brooklyn, and wrestling WWF style with her 15 lb. cat, Weston Cecil. She is a graduate from the American Red Cross Basic Sailing Safety course as well as the University of California, San Diego.

Steve Champeon

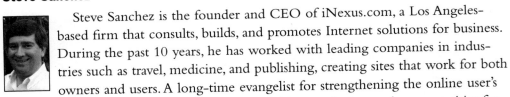

Steve Champeon is CTO at hesketh.com/inc., in Raleigh, North Carolina. The founder and "list mom" of the popular webdesign-L mailing list community, Steve is also author of *Building Dynamic HTML GUIs* (John Wiley & Sons, ©1999), and a contributor to *Cascading Style Sheets: Separating Content from Presentation* (glasshaus, ©2002). In addition, he is the author of dozens of articles on Internet technology and culture. He is an active development and technical editor, with more than two dozen titles to his credit. Steve is a founding member of The Web Standards Project, a grassroots effort to raise the bar on standards support and education. His is a life of many charms, including rocking chairs, iced tea, ceiling fans, Macintoshes, mint juleps, and homemade salsa so hot it would shock you.

Steve Sanchez

Steve Sanchez is the founder and CEO of iNexus.com, a Los Angeles-based firm that consults, builds, and promotes Internet solutions for business. During the past 10 years, he has worked with leading companies in industries such as travel, medicine, and publishing, creating sites that work for both owners and users. A long-time evangelist for strengthening the online user's experience, Steve is a "raving fan" of database-driven web sites, web communities for business, and technologies such as dynamic Flash, VR tours, Active Server Pages, and Microsoft's .NET. He enjoys photography, travel, sailing, and scuba diving. He lives in Los Angeles with his wife and four children.

Acknowledgments

Thanks to Jennifer Eberhardt, my Senior Development Editor, for helping me make this the book I wanted it to be. Thanks to Michael Nolan, my acquisitions editor, for helping me to shape the idea and bring it to New Riders. Thanks to Steve Champeon, Allison Cecil, Chad Brandt, and Steve Sanchez, my technical editors.

Thanks to my associate publisher Stephanie Wall, my production manager Gina Kanouse, my senior product marketing manager Tammy Detrich, my publicity manager Susan Nixon, my senior project editor Sarah Kearns, my copy editor Krista Hansing, and my indexer Lisa Stumpf.

Thanks to all of my colleagues at The New York Public Library, particularly Catherine Jones.

Many thanks to Susan Kaup, David Gasson, Dave Bell, Mark Newhouse, Eric Meyer, Leigh Baker-Foley, Nick Usborne, Kelly Abbott, Luke Tymowski, and Sandee Cohen, for their interviews and advice.

Thanks to Elizabeth Hepola for showing me how to make a web page, and Tanya Rabourn for showing me how to make a web site.

To Susan Hoy, Nadaleen Tempelman-Kluit, Leigh Baker-Foley, Myra LaJoie, Astrid Beck, and Ellen Burton: Thank you for lighting the way.

To my grandparents, Harold and Murriel Bickner: Thanks for making me believe, quite literally, if however briefly, that I was three-quarters Irish Princess.

Tell Us What You Think

As the reader of this book, you are the most important critic and commentator. We value your opinion and want to know what we're doing right, what we could do better, what areas you'd like to see us publish in, and any other words of wisdom you're willing to pass our way.

As the Senior Development Editor for New Riders Publishing, I welcome your comments. You can fax, email, or write me directly to let me know what you did or didn't like about this book—as well as what we can do to make our books stronger. When you write, please be sure to include this book's title, ISBN, and author, as well as your name and phone or fax number. I will carefully review your comments and share them with the author and editors who worked on the book.

Please note that I cannot help you with technical problems related to the topic of this book, and that due to the high volume of email I receive, I might not be able to reply to every message.

Fax: 317-428-3280

Email: jennifer.eberhardt@newriders.com

Mail: Jennifer Eberhardt
         Senior Development Editor
         New Riders Publishing
         800 East 96th Street, 3rd Floor
         Indianapolis, IN 46240 USA

Introduction

You do not need a big budget to build a great web site.

In fact, there are many advantages to working on a tight budget. A well-run, small-budget production can force you to focus on what really matters. The result is a leaner, more effective site whose immediacy enables you to connect with your audience more successfully.

This book is about finding the correct approach to developing great sites on a meager budget. I call this approach *shoestring design*. Throughout these chapters, I'll show you how to apply shoestring design principles to every aspect of web production: project management, usability, design, copywriting, hosting, and post-launch maintenance.

In this book, I share an approach that will not only help you survive tough economic times, but could actually improve your work's quality and usability and enhance your connection with the people who read or use your site. When your economic circumstances improve, you will have developed efficient work habits that help you make the most of larger budgets.

Why Web Design on a Shoestring?

I have a reason for wanting to write this book now, and it is personal. In the heyday of the dot-com era, I worked as a web developer in a large New York City nonprofit. We had some funding that trickled in from time to time, but never much. In 1999, that trickle was to become a constant stream of cash. I was about to realize every small-budget designer's dream. We had secured a budget from my city that was going to boost my staff from 2 to 10; this was to include information architects, graphic designers, editors, writers (what a luxury!), and a few assistants. We were going to conduct a series of large-scale focus groups and usability testing studies over two years. I had designs on a large content-management system and was actually going to have the cash to buy all the support services to move legacy content into the new system. We had planned well, and the budget had anticipated every need for a major expansion. We were ready to spend that money well.

Just as the funds were about to begin rolling in, the stock market tanked. The money that was going to go to my beautiful new web team was reallocated to keeping the doors of our bricks-and-mortar services open. A few months later, New York City took another major hit, the city buckled, and the money was simply gone. It seemed as though all my hopes for an excellent web site were dashed.

The irony is that in the cash-strapped year that followed, we in this two-person office locked ourselves in and accomplished much more than I would have anticipated going into it. With a lean budget, we had to develop a lean attitude.

As we focused on doing small tasks well and keeping organized, our site became gradually more focused. We found ways of making do without formal user studies, by conducting small, informal ones. We paid closer attention to the free user feedback that came from our customers' email messages. We perused our old pages for important content that had been buried, and we spent time refining the language, making it warmer and more conversational.

We skipped the content-management system purchase and built small boutique-size systems that supported a few sections of our site. We developed more efficient workflows. We canned staff meetings that were not productive and killed time-sucking projects.

We did take on new projects, but we were more selective; what we built, we built well. We wrote documentation, learned about and implemented open standards, and instituted other best practices.

After a year of working this way, our site was both more polished and more human than it had been when times were flush.

That is when I realized that I had developed a useful approach to working with small budgets, so I began to write this book. Some of what you will find in these pages comes out of my own experience; other ideas come from shoestring warriors I have spoken with. I hope that these cumulative experiences will help other web professionals who face similar challenges.

As I have traveled the country giving lectures on web design, I have realized that my experience and the shoestring design approach is worth sharing; more of us are working on smaller-budget sites. Many of us work in-house for agencies and nonprofits that have scaled back. Others of us are on our own, working with these very same agencies and nonprofits as clients. With more of us in this boat, I wanted to write a book that would serve as a guide for how to create a wonderful site on a shoestring budget.

Who This Book Is For

Few web developers are working with the budgets we had three or four years ago, but we still have the same responsibilities. This book is for those of us who have seen our budgets abated while our customers' expectations have grown. Essentially, this book is for anyone who has to develop great web sites on a dime. There are many of us in this position: Some are freelancers, others work for small design agencies, and others work as in-house web professionals for large agencies. I have written this book thinking about web professionals from any of these categories. Here are four people who represent our gang of underfunded web professionals.

This book is for John, who is not a full-time web professional but has to produce a site as though he were. John is not a designer, but he is under a lot of pressure from the board of trustees to make a beautiful and robust community portal. He needs to pull off a major redesign in the next six months so that his library looks more up-to-date. The site has an events calendar, but it is currently managed by hand. This takes up too much of his time. John wants to buy, find, or develop an automated tool so that his colleagues can enter data into a web form, and the events calendar will appear on the web automatically. His boss is interested in having an online book discussion for adults and wants John to develop the forum for that. All of this work is to take place in the 17 hours per week during which he is the webmaster. The other part of his time is set aside for his work as a children's librarian.

John's major problem: How can I manage expectations and make the most of the few hours a week that I have to devote to web development?

This book is for Clint, who runs his own one-person web-design shop in Ontario. He attracts clients who are looking for sophisticated design rather than web application development. Clint has been in the field for a number of years, but his list of clients has changed in the last two. Some of those that he did business with are now out of business. The clients that he has retained are short on cash; $20,000 jobs have been replaced by $5,000 jobs, and $10,000 jobs have been replaced by $500 jobs. Clint still loves the medium and wants to produce beautiful sites for his clients, so his approach needs to change. He is looking for ways to deliver beautiful designs and to help his clients cut costs in smart ways. He worries that if he and his clients cut back on the wrong things, they will be spending too much money playing catch-up when finances rebound.

Clint's major problem: How can I help my clients spend their small budgets most effectively and still make money myself?

This book is for Janet, who works in the web office of an insurance agency in Phoenix, Arizona. She is an art school graduate and was once the lead designer on a team that included a few developers, a Flash person, and a project manager. After a round of corporate downsizing, the office consists of Janet, who is responsible for every aspect of web production, and an hourly assistant with no real web experience.

Janet's major problem: How can I do the work of five people?

This book is for Steve, who owns a computer store outside Toledo, Ohio. Steve has volunteered to create, host, and maintain the web site for his 13-year-old daughter's entire baseball league. He lives in a wealthy county, and expectations for the site's look and up-to-date accuracy are high. If the site falls short, he is sure to hear about it from the more difficult yet influential members of the community. Unfortunately for Steve, there is no plan, no budget, and no time to do it.

Steve's major problem: How can I produce a fabulous site in my "free" time?

Shoestring is also for people who have volunteered to create sites for social clubs and religious organizations. It is for anyone who is in the business of making web sites and has little time and money to do it. This book is also for anyone who has a decent budget and wants to make the most of every penny.

What This Book Assumes

Shoestring assumes that you have at least some experience building and publishing web sites. Basic knowledge of (X)HTML is required for some of the chapters. If your knowledge of HTML is limited because you have never made a web site or because you have used only graphical editors such as Dreamweaver or GoLive, you will want to brush up on HTML basics as we go along. You might want to pick up a basic (X)HTML book to have at your side as you read *Shoestring*. I recommend *HTML for the World Wide Web with XHTML and CSS: Visual QuickStart Guide,* Fifth Edition (Peachpit Press, ©1999) by Elizabeth Castro; *XML, HTML, XHTML Magic* (New Riders, ©2001) by Molly E. Holzschlag; or *Designing with Web Standards* (New Riders, ©2003) by Jeffrey Zeldman.

What Is in This Book

Web Design on a Shoestring tackles every aspect of web production from the point of view of a professional who needs to deliver a magnificent site but doesn't have lavish financial resources. Each chapter addresses one of those site production aspects (project planning, user testing, writing, design, content management, HTML markup, and web hosting) and suggests strategies about making the most of it on a shoestring budget.

I have tried to focus on one or two main cost-savings strategies for each chapter, and then to break down these strategies into several techniques that you can put to use immediately.

In Chapter 1, "The Secrets to a Successful Shoestring Project," I give you techniques for keeping your focus clear. This will help keep an otherwise precarious job on track.

In Chapter 2, "The Pound Wise Project Plan," you are encouraged to dare to do less. In preproduction, "less is more" must be the shoestring web professional's mantra. I look at ways to simplify your project plan and to manage expectations that, if unchecked, can eat up your budget.

Chapter 3, "Usability on the Cheap," focuses on how to use small, informal user studies early and often, and on how to create a toolkit of usability techniques that become part of your web development repertoire. You don't have to spend much to have your site benefit tremendously from good usability.

Chapter 4, "Why Good Copy Counts," should convince you that the savvy shoe-string professional takes advantage of good copy. Words are the only aspect of a site that you have complete control over, and they can either elevate or bring down your site. Good copy can also be repurposed for newsletters and other free and inexpensive marketing tools. I look at ways to write well for the web without spending too much money, and show you how to maximize the value of every word.

Chapter 5, "The Design: Looking Good with Less," is about solid design on a small budget. You might not have the money for expensive stock art or top-notch graphic designers, but if you define your style and stick to it, and keep the colors, lines, and typography clean, you can produce an inexpensive site that looks like a million bucks.

Even shoestring web professionals have to manage large content properties. Our work is not limited to small boutique sites. Managing all that content can be expensive if you do it manually, but a content-management system (CMS) can also be expensive. In Chapter 6, "Content Management on a Tight Budget," I show you how to find the best CMS for your dime (or for free).

The shoestring professional must do important behind-the-screens work to save time and money on site maintenance, storage, server costs, and even accessibility. In Chapter 7, "Save Time and Money with Web Standards," I look at the underpinnings of a well-constructed, durable web site that will save big bucks in the long run.

So you've built a site, but now you need to find an affordable way to serve it. In Chapter 8, "Bang-for-Your-Buck Hosting and Domains," I show you how to find good value in hosting and domain name services, and how to put together a good defense against some of the hidden costs that too often accompany domain and hosting services.

How to Use This Book

It is my hope that you will write in this book, dog-ear a few pages, and splash coffee on the cover. Treat it with little reverence. Let it become an old friend that you can lean on from time to time. Ignore the stuff you don't need, and enjoy the parts that help.

You'll find that each chapter begins with a "Chapter Checklist." Use these checklists as guidelines to help you move more efficiently through the chapters.

Short sections called "Spinning Straw into Gold" punctuate the book; these sections highlight approaches to the money-saving aspects introduced in each chapter. I have also defined terms and phrases throughout this book; skim the sidebars to familiarize yourself with new terms and concepts.

The "Budget Threat" sections in each chapter identify potential hazards to your limited supply of funds. As in life, emergency spending can quickly clear out your bank account. Fortunately, web site budget threats are a little easier to predict than flooded basements or unexpected veterinary bills. I hope that the "Budget Threat" highlights will help you avoid extra expenses.

Shoestring is not cumulative; you do not need to read Chapter 1 to understand Chapter 2, so feel free to jump around and go at your own pace. You can skip around to the issues that you face now, or you can read it from start to finish. If you are in a hurry, you might want at first to take a superficial pass at a chapter. Read the checklist, and review the "Budget Threat" and "Spinning Straw into Gold" blurbs. Then when you have time, come back and read the chapter in full. I have designed the book for busy people, and even a quick skim should help you move forward in your work.

Begin by Doing Less

If you are reading this book, you are probably short on time as well as money, so I want to jump right in. The trick to making a shoestring budget work is to do less and do it well. If you do not have the money for a full-blown content-management system, select one that does 80% of what a CMS should do, but one that does that 80% well. If you have a tight budget for stock art, use fewer photographs, but make sure the ones you buy are terrific.

As you move forward, keep one principle in mind:

Dare to do less.

Part I:

Production

Chapter 1

The Secrets to a Successful Shoestring Project

Chapter Checklist

1. **Use the resources at hand.**

   You probably have resources at your disposal that you have not tapped yet. I'll show you how to see what you have—hardware, software, design tools, or talented people—and use it effectively.

2. **Involve a relatively small group of decision makers.**

   Committees and boards are terrific for some things, such as brainstorming for new ideas. But you must be careful to keep all decision making in the hands of a small, consistent group. This will help maintain your focus, and it will help you save money by cutting down on the time that it takes to make a decision.

3. **Have a clear focus.**

   Know what you want out of your site. If this is a small-budget temporary measure for something that will be expanded later, give your team a sense of what goes in this limited phase and what gets saved for the next iteration.

4. **Dare to do less.**

   Relax, you do not have to do everything! If you have a small site, set smaller goals. Concentrate on doing a few things well.

> *No, I'm from Iowa; I work in outer space.*

—William Shatner as James T. Kirk in *Star Trek IV: The Voyage Home* (1986)

There is no perfect way to produce a successful shoestring site. I would love to say, "Never pay more than 24 doubloons for a content-management system" or "Always dedicate at least one-third of your budget to interface design." The fact is, there are many ways to build a site—and even more ways to spend money.

But successful shoestring sites share four common elements—a successful shoestring site always...

1. Uses the resources at hand.
2. Is managed by a relatively small group of decision makers.
3. Has a clear focus.
4. Dares to do less.

In the next two sections, I take a look at a few sites that share these elements.

Astronomy Education Review

In 2001, three web developers from the National Optical Astronomy Observatory—David Gasson, Dave Bell, and Mark Newhouse—set about creating the first and only professional, refereed education journal dedicated to astronomy. The site was Astronomy Education Review (http://aer.noao.edu/), and they did all the work in-house, without a penny of extra funding (see Figures 1.1 and 1.2).

> *"We were careful to be very explicit about the initial scope of the project, and to design the database in such a way that it could be expanded in the future as time, money, and inclination allowed."*
>
> —David Gasson

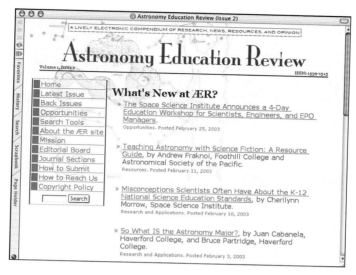

1.1 *Astronomy Education Review (*`http://aer.noao.edu/`*) is the first and only professional, refereed education journal dedicated to astronomy. The site was started with no budget, but it was such a success that the development team was awarded a large grant from NASA to continue the project.*

1.2 *The Astronomy Education Review team.*
Pictured are David Gasson, Mark Newhouse, and Dave Bell.

The team used a strategy that is colloquially called MAP, which stands for MySQL, Apache, and Perl or PHP. These are all free, open source software:

- **MySQL**—The team used MySQL (www.mysql.com) as the database back end that holds all the site's content.
- **Apache**—AER runs on an Apache server (www.apache.org), with FreeBSD (www.freebsd.org) working as the server software.
- **Perl and PHP Server**—All the server-side scripting is done with a combination of Perl and PHP (www.php.net). This is the glue that connects the content in the database to the web pages that the client sees.

Talk about using the resources at hand! Open source software can be a splendid way to develop a site with sophisticated functional requirements, and you can do it without spending a fortune. In the case of AER, this small, inexpensive site grew into more opportunities for the team.

When Astronomy Education Review launched in October 2002, the first submissions were from close peers and colleagues, and the editorial board was a group of volunteers. After the first few issues were released, articles from other scientists started to pour in. Now there is a steady stream of content.

Recently, NASA offered Astronomy Education Review $150,000 over two years in support of the journal, and the site continues to receive recognition as a place to go for the latest information in the astronomy education community.

The team at the National Optical Astronomy Observatory created a successful new site by using what free resources were at hand.

Leigh Baker-Foley: NotLimited NYC, LLC

Leigh Baker–Foley of NotLimited NYC, LLC (see Figure 1.3) recently created a site for Richard Ronco Woodworking (`www.nodltd.com/ronco/`), shown in Figure 1.4. She delivered this project for a budget of about $2,500.

1.3 *NotLimited NYC, LLC, is one of many small agencies whose bread-and-butter gigs are shoestring projects. The company's principal, Baker-Foley, works with clients who have discovered that less can (and must) equal much, much more in financial and visitor returns. Designers who can deliver what Baker-Foley describes as "pared-down, beautiful, and functional sites" are those who are best positioned to produce beautiful work and keep food on the table. Baker-Foley has learned to create valuable sites and a sustainable company from thin air.*

1.4 *One of Baker-Foley's recent projects was to create a web site for a small, high-end woodworking shop in Bangor, Maine (see* http://nodltd.com/ronco/). *Baker-Foley saved money for the client by keeping the site simple, creating the photography herself, using standards-compliant markup, and self-hosting the site.*

The success of this project depended on two things:

1. The client and designer were specific about their priorities. When you have a small budget, some things have to go.

2. The concept of the site was clear. When I asked Baker-Foley how she kept the budget for the RRW site so low, she outlined her approach:

   □ **Keep the site layout and architecture simple and extensible.** The simplicity of the layout and GUI of this site was inspired by the elegant understatement of the RRW's own product. Later, when the client is ready, an easily extensible site is already in place that will accommodate additional galleries and new informational pages. This new work can be done without additional design costs.

   □ **Develop the content with the client.** The content was based on conversations with the client, as well as from additional research of the content that the client felt was missing from competitors' sites. This eliminated outside fees for additional copywriting and editing.

- **Create all graphics and photographs in-house.** All photographs, graphics, and even the client brand were created and designed in-house as part of the job spec, saving RRW all costs of stock imagery, art, and photography.

- **Program the entire site in standards-compliant XHTML and CSS.** The use of standards-compliant code for page display and CSS for layout not only ensures current and future compatibility and legibility across platforms and browsers. It also equates to vast savings in additional future programming and site updates because of its universal accessibility and ease of use to even the most intermediate site programmers. See Chapter 7, "Save Time and Money with Web Standards."

- **Host the finished site on an existing account.** By using space on her professional site, Baker-Foley was able to offer the client inexpensive hosting and save RRW the cost of domain registration. The site looks fabulous, and because of its standards-oriented construction, the weight in kilobytes per second is negligible; it was well worth the trade-off.

RRW's is an encouraging story for a number of reasons. For one thing, following the first characteristic of a successful shoestring site, the project takes advantage of the resources at hand. The designer had a decent digital camera and took photographs of the client's work. (We talk about how to make the most of photography in Chapter 5, "The Design: Looking Good with Less.")

Second, the project anticipates a time when resources might be more flush. As the woodworking business grows, the architecture of the site will be flexible enough to add new galleries of Ronco's work. As we talk about in Chapter 7, the site also takes advantage of the economy afforded by using good structural markup that is styled with Cascading Style Sheets. This saves time and money on production, redesign, hosting, and serving.

One last thing that I love is that this site is hosted within the NotLimited domain itself. This keeps the client's hosting costs down for now. Later, when budgets increase, RRW can license its own domain and be hosted independently.

The success of any shoestring project hinges on deciding what you want to spend your limited resources on now and what you can do later when budgets grow. In the case of RRW, the client and designer were explicit about what to focus on now to make this site a success.

What Makes a Successful Shoestring Site?

Now that you've seen how a couple of real-world sites have dealt with working on a shoestring, let's dive into the specifics.

Take Advantage of the Resources at Hand

An apocryphal tale tells of Martha Washington and socks. The story goes that she made a gown out of the threads from George's old socks. She unraveled each stocking, wove the string into cloth, and made her dress from that cloth.

I am not suggesting that we turn to our tube socks collection to build splendid sites, but I do think that there are assets around each of us that can be put to use in resourceful ways. The way that Baker-Foley used her consumer digital camera to photograph Ronco's work is a perfect example; I'll look at many more ways to use what you have to create beautiful but inexpensive web sites.

Spinning Straw into Gold

Being a web professional is not the lucrative occupation it used to be. There are fewer jobs, and you are not likely to get rich making web pages. But the people who are doing extraordinary work and who are bringing home the bacon have learned to take advantage of lean times. People specializing in small, inexpensive sites that work wonderfully have a special value to bring to their companies, bosses, and clients. One of the things that I hope to do with this book is share techniques and tricks that will make you one of these valuable workers who can spin straw into gold.

Keep the Number of Decision Makers Small

Just before *The Wizard of Oz* was released in 1939, MGM studio executives nearly cut "Somewhere Over the Rainbow" from the film. They felt that the song was a bit slow and that it made the film drag. The song was allowed to stay, but it chills me to the bone when I think that this almost happened. Did they consider killing the ruby-red slippers as well? This is the kind of threat that all creative projects face: Too many decision makers can kill a project by watering down decision-making processes.

David Ogilvy, one of the fathers of modern advertising and the author of some of the most delicious quotations of the twentieth century (do a Google search on "Ogilvy quotations"), once wrote, "Much of the messy advertising you see on television today is the product of committees. Committees can criticize advertisements, but they should never be allowed to create them."

The same must be said of web sites. The least successful sites that I ever participated in all had navigational schemes, site names, or color palates that were created by committees. When faced with a creative task, committees bring out the mediocrity in every participant. Good ideas get watered down. Serious problems are often left unattended. Projects lose focus as the best parts of several ideas become a messy goop of a web site. I would rather see one person or team take a flawed approach to building a site than to see a committee work on a better approach. The small team working on the flawed approach will be more likely to deliver a project with focus, and to deliver it on time.

The Site Must Have One Focus

I used to teach academic writing to college students, and the best papers were not necessarily those with the greatest breadth, but those with the least ambiguous focus. Some students wrote papers with what I called a machine gun approach: They tried to cover every idea introduced in a semester, thinking that if they were to spray their paper with lots of facts, one bullet might hit the mark. These papers were not good. The best papers were those that followed one idea, even a slightly flawed idea, through a focused, sustained discussion.

What distinguishes good papers from bad is the same thing that distinguishes successful sites from unsuccessful sites: focus.

Focus is especially important when your staffing resources are slim. I once joined a project in which work had been driven by two competing concepts of the project. Work followed one concept for a while, and then another concept took over. Developers, designers, and writers worked in circles, never sure of which master to serve. Months of labor were wasted simply because the project lacked focus.

Eventually, the project concept was clarified. Within months we were able to produce what had not been accomplished in a year of work. Morale improved, and that helped our productivity even more.

This was a relatively large project, and these costs were "absorbed" into a cushy budget. But lack of focus is the kiss of death for a small project; there is no place to hide inefficiency.

Having a definite focus also helps you achieve short- and long-term goals. Leigh Baker-Foley helped her woodworking client make good short- and long-term decisions. Remember that RRW did not register a domain name, but instead elected to have the site reside in a subdirectory of Leigh's business site. That bit of savings over the course of a year might be enough to hire a photographer or to add a new gallery to the site. Whether you are in a client/consultant relationship or are working as an in-house web developer for a company, keeping a good grip on your long-term goals will help make your short-term efforts pay off and will give you more satisfaction as you deliver work on the initial phase of the project.

The Project Must Dare to Do Less

I love the films of director Jim Jarmusch. Part of my admiration comes from the fact that he exercises a restraint that I like to use when I build web sites. I once heard him interviewed about his film *Down By Law*. He was discussing the way he lets a sense of place shape his films. Rather than use over-the-top landmarks or clichés to loudly say, "Yo, this is New Orleans," he lets place seep into the films in a light-handed way. There are no shots of Café Du Monde or Mardi Gras in his films; he will not hammer his viewers over the head like that. Instead, Jarmusch lets you slowly soak up the mood of the city by showing you interior shots of anonymous run-down buildings at unspecified locations. This restraint lends a sense of calm and elegance to his low-budget pictures. When you have a small budget, it is best to use restraint.

"Dare to do less" is a phrase I heard Tim Bray, one of the authors of XML, use when he gave a talk on the predictors for successful technology. When you look at all of the new technologies that are hitting the market, how do you predict which technologies will succeed? Bray has found that one of the best predictors of success is that a technology does one or two things well. Technologies that try to do all things for all people tend to fail.

This book is not about developing new technologies, but web developers can take away a lesson from Bray's idea: Create sites that do one or two things well, and don't worry about every possible feature or function. This book is about creating web sites that dare to do less so that you, your clients, your colleagues, and especially your users can have more.

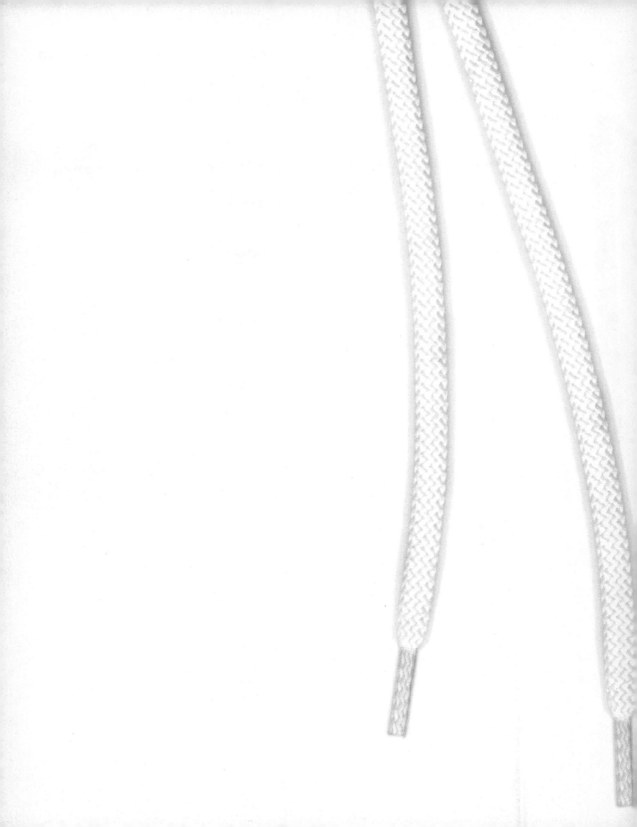

Chapter 2

The Pound Wise Project Plan

Chapter Checklist

1. **Dare to do less.**

   It will be tempting to load up your project with every wonderful idea that occurs to you and your colleagues. Remember that your budget is small; you are better off if you scale back and do a few things well. Save the expensive ideas for a later phase of production.

2. **Write a short project goals document.**

   If your project plan is vague, your small budget will be eaten up by indecision, rethinking, and patch-up work. Make sure that you start the job with a clear project goals document.

3. **Create a functional requirements document.**

   It pays to be explicit about each of the functional requirements for the site. If you do not have a list of functional requirements in place, you will pay through the nose, wasting time and money on production work that you don't need.

4. **Craft a technical requirements document.**

   Take the time to list technical requirements such as target browsers and system specifications, and use this list to test the site as you build it. If you wait until it's finished to test it against your technical benchmarks, your changes and bug fixes will cost far more than they have to. Never put yourself in a position where you have to pay for expensive post-production fixes to easily avoidable problems.

5. **Keep documentation nearby.**

   It is important not only to write project goals and functional and technical requirements, but also to read them—and make sure your colleagues read them, too. I like to keep this documentation short and pin it to the bulletin board, where it serves as a constant reminder of what I'm trying to achieve.

> *Oh, I realize it's a penny here and a penny there, but look at me: I've worked myself up from nothing to a state of extreme poverty.*
>
> —Groucho Marx in *Monkey Business* (1931)

The promise of this book is to show you how to build a wonderful site on a shoe-string budget. Although these pages share important techniques for working through each phase and aspect of a shoestring site, the overall success of your project depends on the planning work that you do at the outset. After all, the success of any project is the result of good organization and a straightforward concept. This is especially true for shoestring sites. When you have little money, you can't afford to take on the bloat that accompanies ill-defined goals and poorly organized work plans.

This bloat often goes unnoticed in big-budget sites. Larger budgets afford web professionals more opportunity for indecision and lack of direction. An unclear path leads to a major eleventh-hour revision; labor is wasted on last-minute fixes for problems that could have been avoided through better planning.

One of the pleasures of working on a dime a day is that you are required to run lean. Shoestring web professionals, forced to take a focused, stripped-down approach to a project, are a bit like adventure travelers who can't afford to pack their rucksacks with frivolities. The planning phase of web site production is like packing for a trip. When you plan for a small-budget site, you need to be selective about what goals and requirements you bring along.

Careful Planning Pays

In 1996, mountaineer Rob Hall led a team of climbers on what turned out to be a disastrous expedition to the top of Mount Everest. Commercial tourism was big business, and what were arguably underqualified climbers had been able to buy a trip up what was becoming an overcrowded mountain. One such climber, a wealthy socialite, brought an espresso maker along on the expedition. She survived the journey—no thanks to the extra weight she was toting, which at such altitudes and temperatures posed a serious and foolish risk. But the lady and her coffeemaker became a symbol of the excess that commercial Everest tours had become. That espresso maker is exactly what web professionals need to look out for as they approach web sites with limited budgets.

Overstuffed backpacks have undermined many sites, no matter what the budget is. Before any journey, it is tempting to load up on all of the fabulous things that you might use. But low-budget travelers must pack with care. Think of your shoestring site's development as a trip up a tall mountain, where any bit of extra weight is a burden that you have to carry. Pack too much, and it will cost you.

I have never done any mountaineering, but I used to rock-climb. Most of my crag time took place in a climbing gym. My climbing friends and I scaled 70-foot slabs made of plywood and synthetic rock formations. The gym was pricey, and I think it made most of its money by selling beverages. Bottled water was about $3 a pop. These were my graduate student days, and I did not have money for extras, so I brought tap water from home. Pretty simple stuff, but I probably saved hundreds of dollars each year that I climbed there.

Budget Threat: Treating Small-Budget Sites Too Casually Can Be Expensive

I have enjoyed a modest supplemental income from creating small-budget sites in my free time. I learned the hard way that neglecting the planning phase of such a site costs money in the long run. By failing to plan and budget for basic things, such as the cost of new fonts, the time to produce web-ready images, and the labor of authoring content that was supposed to have been created by someone else, I have worked more hours without pay than I care to add up. Whether you are working freelance, in an agency, or in-house, don't let poor planning eat away at your budget this way.

So often when web professionals approach a small site, they don't take the time to plan. A low dollar amount can lead people to think, "This is a minor project that I can do in my off hours. It is a casual job that will evolve on its own." Don't ever put yourself in this position! You will pay dearly for taking that attitude. If you are working on a flat fee, you will not recover your costs. If you are working on a billable-hour schedule and you pass that cost on to the client, shame on you! If you are working full-time as part of an in-house team, you will pay personally by working late and on weekends to make up for time lost to lack of vision. One way or another, lack of planning will cost you big-time.

An Ounce of Prevention

If you plan well, your project has a better chance of staying on budget. Specifically, you need to address three steps formally and rigorously:

1. Define the goals of your site.
2. Define the functional requirements.
3. Define the technical requirements.

None of these steps needs to be overly involved, but you do have to take the time to write each definition in a document. These documents will help you and your budget stay on track.

Budget Threat: Scope Creep

An unstoppable phenomenon is common to all web sites: scope creep. The development of a web site is hard to pin down. New ideas surface, and needs change. The scope of your project expands exponentially as new ideas and new "needs" are added. Scope creep can be good or bad, depending on how you manage it. The trick is to direct these shifts by making conscientious adjustments to the definition of your site and by carefully adjusting the budget to fit the new needs. Clearly defined project goals and carefully articulated functional and technical requirements will help you stay sane and in the black as you begin to experience scope creep.

Shoestring Project Goals

Before you begin to work, sit down and take the time to write out what you are trying to achieve with your site. Let's work with a hypothetical example. The following is a freelance scenario, but the principles apply to any web–development circumstance.

Sample Site: Project Goals for the Something Blue Site

Imagine that an artist, Mary Hoy, has asked you to create a site based on her last exhibition, Something Blue. She can pay only a pittance. You like her work and figure that a pittance will help pay the bills, so you take her on as a client. Mary has never been involved in web site creation, so has no way of shaping the scope of the site. You correctly anticipate that her lack of experience might lead her to change her goals and requirements over time. When she sees what her work looks like on the web, she'll be inspired to try new ideas or to add functional requirements to the site. You have anticipated these problems. To protect yourself and the budget, you formalize the project's goals:

Project Goals for the Something Blue Web Site

Something Blue will be an online exhibition of the works of artist Mary Hoy. The site will include 15 of the 40 images in her bricks-and-mortar exhibition (also called Something Blue) that took place at the Good Girl Gallery in Studio City, California, in July 2003. In addition to the 15 images, the site will include 2 interviews with the artist, her resume, and her contact information. The purpose of the site is primarily to promote her work, to give Hoy an online "calling card," and perhaps to lead to a sale or two, although no selling will be done directly on the site.

This is a good example of a budget-sensitive project goal document because it is specific. First, you have established the *genre* of the site: This is an exhibition, not a retrospective or an e-commerce site. Second, you have quantified the scope of the project. The difference in the cost of producing 15 scans versus 40 scans might add up to quite a bit. You are probably going to be the one doing the scanning and the image editing. This will take time, and creating a schedule around a specific number of images will help you stay on track both for the schedule and the bottom line. The same is true for the interviews and the contact information; you can anticipate the number of web pages that you will have to build. As you put your budget together, you can attach a dollar amount to each major site element.

Budget Threat: Keep the Number of Decision Makers Small

As explained in Chapter 1, "The Secrets to a Successful Shoestring Project," one of the secrets to creating a successful shoestring web site is to keep the number of decision makers small. The more people you involve in the goal-setting phase, the more diffuse your project goals might be. Good resource allocation requires a carefully defined project. If a large group of decision makers is keeping you from nailing down the project goals early in the game, try to pare the number of decision makers to a few key people. If you don't, you will spend big bucks on unfocused work that goes nowhere.

The project goals document cannot save your budget or your sanity if it is not shared with the site's stakeholders. In the Something Blue scenario, the only decision maker is your client, Mary. Most sites, however, involve more stakeholders. You must communicate with all your stakeholders without turning them all into decision makers. The more levels of approval that are required to get the site moving, the more involved and expensive the process will be. More important, the more people are involved in a creative process, the more diffuse the focus can become. Distinguishing between stakeholders and decision makers is not a license to be cavalier; don't blow off the big wigs because, if you ignore them up front, they will be inclined to kill your project just before it launches. Talk about a waste of time and money! Make sure that your group of decision makers is small, but be politic in selecting the composition of that group.

> **Definition: Client**
>
> In this book, I use the term *client* to refer to anyone who has engaged you for web production. This could be a single client who has hired you to do freelance work, your direct supervisor, or in-house colleagues who depend on you to develop the company's site.

When you have formally established your group of decision makers, be sure to share the project goals document with the whole gang. It *does not* matter whether they are clients or colleagues. It *does* matter that you all agree on the goals of the site. If the goals change later, someone will have to pay for the extra time and materials; if you have formal sign-off from clients, colleagues, and bosses, you lessen your chances of getting stuck with the tab.

A formal document that nails down the initial scope places you in a much better position to ask for more resources when, for example, artist Mary Hoy decides that she wants 30, not 15, images of her work. You should never have to pay the price when someone else has a change of mind.

Nail Down the Functional Requirements Early

Establishing goals is the best way to keep control of a shoestring site, but you need to buttress that work with clearly defined functional requirements.

Let's return to Mary's Something Blue site again and create a functional requirements document. Again, this example assumes that you are a freelance web professional, but the same process can and should be applied by professionals working in any environment. You can start by interviewing your client about what she wants the site to do. The result of your interview will be a broad wish list that might include the following:

- I would like my visitors to be able to search the site for images and, when they click on them, be able to zoom in and see each piece, down to the detail of the paint strokes.
- My users need to be able to scan the images quickly and then pick the image that they want to see in more detail.
- My mother has a slow dial-up connection to the web, and I want her to be able to look at my site. I hate sites that take a long time to load.
- It must be easy for users to contact me; I want them to be able to call or send me an email if they want to buy a piece or show my art.

Clearly, not every item on such a wish list will make it onto a site with such a small budget. Your job as the web professional is to let the client know that you have heard all of her ideas and that you take them seriously, and to pare the wish list to a set of functional requirements that can be delivered on budget. You'll need to massage the wish list into a functional requirements document that can be accommodated by the resources at hand.

The result of this message should look something like this:

Functional Requirements for the Something Blue Web Site, Version One

The Something Blue web site has possibilities that are broad and exciting, but a few of these are too ambitious for the initial launch. Taken all at once, the potential requirements would result in a budget that exceeds the resources at hand. We have boiled them down to a few complementary requirements that can be achieved within the current budget and timeline. Some of the more expensive requirements that did not make it into this proposal should be saved for a second iteration of the site.

Requirement	Notes	Cost
Users must be able to click on a small version of an image to see a larger image. The larger image will be about 600 pixels wide, a size that accommodates most computer screens.	This is an economically viable alternative to the desired pan and zoom technology that would allow users to zoom into each image. It will not allow users to zoom into such detail as paint strokes, but it will afford a nice size of viewing area. An added benefit of this alternative is that users with slow Internet connections will not be forced to view the large image unless they choose to.	$
Users must be able to quickly scan all images by scrolling through a strip of small thumbnail-size images.		$
The site must be quick-loading and easy to use on a slow Internet connection.		$
Users must have quick access to contact information.		$

Possible Requirements for Next Phase of Web Development

The site must have a search engine.	This could be expensive and might not be necessary now because you are working with such a small number of images. But you can make this an item for another phase of production, perhaps when you add many more images to the site later.

Note this well: If you can't get your client to scale back the requirements to fit the budget, this is your chance to walk away. Nailing down an unambiguous vision of what will and will not be on the site is absolutely essential. If you can't get there, everyone will be unhappy in the end. You will work long hours that you will not get paid for, and your final deliverable will not satisfy your client.

I can't emphasize enough that the most important factor in creating a site on a shoestring budget is to consciously restrict the scope to include a limited set of achievable functional requirements. Remember that less is more; it is much better to do a few things well than to try to do too many things and fail.

Spinning Straw into Gold

Even with a big budget, you will find it hard to include every item on a client's wish list. Knowing which requirements to table for the short term will help you deliver focused sites on time and on budget. The items that you table for a second iteration might butter your bread later. A happy client might call you in the future when she has more cash to expand her site. Many freelance web professionals are staying in business these days by working with long-term clients who provide a steady, if small, stream of work. Help yourself develop a list of clients like this, and you might begin to enjoy a little stability.

Every time you are asked to expand or change the scope of your site, pull out the functional requirements document upon which you and the client agreed, and discuss how you might best modify this list to accommodate the new request. You might need to drop one requirement for another. Let the client know about these trade-offs, and ask her to help you evaluate them. This is also your time to talk about the additional resources that are necessary to add to the list.

As discussed earlier, the scope of your site might change as work progresses. If Mary the artist tells you at the halfway point that she also wanted to sell art from the Something Blue site and now she needs a shopping cart, you will be able to show her what this change means to her bottom line.

Each time a client change compels you to modify the functional requirements document, give the document a new version number. Keep the older versions of the document so that you can see how the project is evolving (or devolving). If version four of the document differs significantly from version one, make sure you have the resources to carry out the project as it has come to be defined.

Often the new ideas that clients and bosses come up with will be easy to accommodate, and you will not have to ask for more resources. Update the document anyway, adjust the version number, and make sure your client or boss sees it. If you do this consistently, the client will at least understand that all changes to the scope of the project must be acknowledged formally. This will also discourage frivolous changes and help keep you from having to pay the price for scope creep.

Establish Your Technical Requirements

Defining your technical requirements early is just as important of a money-saving device as defining your project goal or functional requirements. In the first years of my career as a web professional, I worked on a few sites whose technical requirements were left vague. This lack of clear technical requirements sometimes came back to haunt us. In one instance, we hired a consultant who developed a beautiful site for us. The site was wonderful in the current version of the Netscape browser, but it broke when we viewed it in Internet Explorer. Our target browsers had not been formally identified, and the consultant had assumed that the site needed to work only on Netscape. (As you can tell, this is not a recent story.) After a little tooth pulling, our consultant adjusted his markup and code so the site would work on a wider set of browsers. He also picked up the bill for the extra hours of labor. If we had defined our target browsers early, however, he would have saved time and money, and we would have saved the administrative overhead that was required to facilitate the fix.

Clearly defined technical requirements can keep you from burning up your budget on these kinds of post-production fixes. Explain your needs simply, in plain English. When you have created this language, you can use it again in subsequent Requests for Proposal (RFP) and other web-development documents.

If you are a client, make sure that you turn in this information to your vendor. If you are the vendor, you might have to help your client determine technical requirements. The initial work might seem time-consuming, but it will save heaps of time and money in the long run. Here are some technical requirements that I have been using that have successfully saved me time, money, and stress.

Technical Requirements Checklist

Some of the items that should be included on your technical requirements document include these:

- ☐ **Target browsers and operating systems**—Do you care about 4.0 browsers? Only modern browsers? Handheld devices? Do you care whether your site works on a PC, or are your users on Macs? Be sure to list these receiving devices explicitly, accurately, and carefully. Use this list to test browser performance as you go. (Don't wait until the project is finished to test it in the targeted browsers and devices. Fixing problems that late in the game is far more costly than spotting them earlier in the process.)

- ☐ **HTML and CSS**—Do you have a particular HTML and Cascading Style Sheet specification in mind? (Hint: The answer is "yes." I go over this topic and how it can save you money in Chapter 7, "Save Time and Money with Web Standards.")

- ☐ **Scripting**—Be explicit about how your professionals should use JavaScript. I personally believe that every function must work when JavaScript is turned off. This keeps a broader range of users happy, including those who lack access to JavaScript-capable browsers.

- ☐ **Servers and databases**—Make sure that you are explicit about the server on which the site will run, and the middleware and database applications that are supported.

- ☐ **Bandwidth requirements**—Take the time to determine whether your audience is primarily using low- or high-speed Internet connections. If most are on some kind of broadband connection such as DSL or cable, you will not have to worry about speed optimization as much as you would if most users were on dial-up connections. On intranets, everyone might be on the same high-speed network. With public sites, as of this writing, at least half of your visitors are likely to be at dial-up speeds of 56K and less. Web Site Optimization's free online bandwidth report keeps track of public connection speeds at work and at home (www.websiteoptimization.com/bw/).

After conducting a survey based on this checklist, it's time to sit down and write your technical requirements document. Keep it short, sweet, and easy to read. Listing the technical requirements formally will protect you from paying for development that you can't use. The specifications discussed in the following chapters are not comprehensive; they are simply examples that are intended to get you thinking about these cost-sensitive issues.

Good Planning Pays

Now that you have your project goals, functional requirements, and technical requirements in place, you are ready to begin production. Your life will be much easier and your work much more efficient because you have taken the time to plan. You will have to make adjustments as you go, but with each shift you'll create good documentation. This will help you ask for more resources if you need them and will help you better allocate the resources that you do have.

This chapter is only the tip of the iceberg; there is much more to learn and discuss about site planning and the web production process. I have given you a few tools that will help you move into production, but if you have more time for study, I highly recommend *Web ReDesign: Workflow that Works* (New Riders Publishing, 2001), by Kelly Goto and Emily Cotler.

Chapter 3

Usability on the Cheap

Chapter Checklist

1. **Usability on the cheap.**

   The key to keeping usability and user testing an affordable part of a shoestring web project is to integrate these concerns into the project early and to develop good interface habits that become part of your everyday toolkit.

2. **Thrifty user testing.**

   Conduct small-scale tests early and often. Your motto should be, "Lather, rinse, repeat." With each design iteration, test!

3. **Keep it simple.**

   Using the sample user study discussed later in this chapter as a guide, gather a few potential users and ask them to perform specific tasks. Don't think of this as a time-consuming ordeal: Writing the script, interviewing a handful of friends or colleagues, and analyzing the results will take an afternoon, at most.

4. **Shoestring usability toolkit.**

   Those of us working with limited budgets need to become expert or at least semi-expert in many areas of web site production, including usability. If this is not your area of strength, invest in learning the basics. Review the interface design tips outlined in this chapter. Take time to expand your knowledge. You will use these principles repeatedly, and the time you invest now will pay off for years to come. Of books that can help you learn more about usability, I recommend Steve Krug's *Don't Make Me Think!* (Que, 2000).

5. **Recyclable HTML library**

   The way you write markup has a profound effect on your site's usability and its accessibility for people with disabilities. Creating good markup can sometimes take more time up front than creating bad markup; but if you begin to create a library of good material, you can leverage this work on future projects. You will also see a tremendous return on investment as you become more efficient at writing polished markup and as your sites become usable to an ever-widening audience.

> ❝❝*Generosity lies less in giving much than in giving at the right moment.*❞❞

—Jean De La Bruyére (1645–1696)

This chapter shows you how to make the most of usability and user testing on a small budget. This is an area where, if resources permit, you can blow the wad. To avoid budget burn, shoestring web professionals must address this important aspect of web site production with a conservative, carefully measured strategy. This strategy should consist of three parts:

1. Conduct small, informal user studies early and often.
2. Create a toolkit of usability techniques that become part of your web-development repertoire.
3. Develop a library of user-friendly and accessible HTML markup components that you can use repeatedly.

Definition: Web Usability

You'll find more flavors of web usability than there are of Methodism, so as I pin down this term, I am sure to offend some people's understanding of the art and science of web usability. But I find it handy to work with a simple definition: Web usability is the practice of making a site's navigation and functionality intuitive.

Usability gives you a choice in how you want your users to expend their mental energy. Do you want them to expend it learning how to move around your site, or do you want them to expend it enjoying and interacting with your site's content? The answer should be obvious. This is a book about economy, a principle that should be applied to your user experience as well as your pocketbook.

Definition: User Testing

User testing is nothing new, nor is it unique to the web. When you develop any product, whether it is a telephone system, a tea kettle, or a web site, it helps to have real, live users work with the product before you send it out the door. By watching humans respond to your site, you uncover flaws that you, being too involved in the product, are blind to. A wonderful introduction to usability and user testing is Donald Norman's *The Design of Everyday Things* (Basic Books, 2002).

Two or three years ago, web site teams included usability experts who were responsible for distinct deliverables to the other members of the team. Developers delivered code, designers delivered templates, and usability engineers (as they were sometimes called) conducted user tests and were often responsible for the overall user experience of a site.

If you have the good fortune of being able to afford staff whose sole responsibility is usability, wonderful! Take advantage of this precious resource! But as we discussed in the introduction of this book, most shoestring web sites (and, for that matter, many other sites) do not have a budget that accommodates specialists. Shoestring web professionals tend to be generalists who are responsible for more than one aspect of production. If you have bothered to pick up this book, chances are good that you are one of those lucky people who are responsible for web site usability, but you do not have the background or budget to give this important area all that it deserves. The three-part strategy listed previously will help you keep usability on the front burner without having to work too many extra hours or spend too much money.

Thrifty User Testing

User testing is one area in which you can spend quite a bit of money if you have it: You can hire a firm that specializes in this area, or you can set up a usability lab with video cameras and other gear to monitor sample user groups as they browse your site or attempt to perform specific tasks within it. But if you are working on a shoestring budget, you will have to find another way to address usability.

My parents met as juniors at the University of Detroit in 1965. Their courtship was modest: My dad usually took my mom out for tea and saltines. After the feast, it was college hoops. The dates were not fancy, but they worked. Two years later, my folks got hitched. Today they are still together and happy. Sure, if the dates had been better funded, they might have seen more of the city, but the basketball and crackers were enough for them to spend time together, get to know one another, and realize that they were on to something good. The recipe for successful talking is the same for user testing.

Do Small Tests Early

Even when your site plans consist of scribbles on napkins (see Figure 3.1), it is not too early to begin to conduct user testing. As soon as you have ideas about the shape and organization of your site, you can collect feedback from potential users.

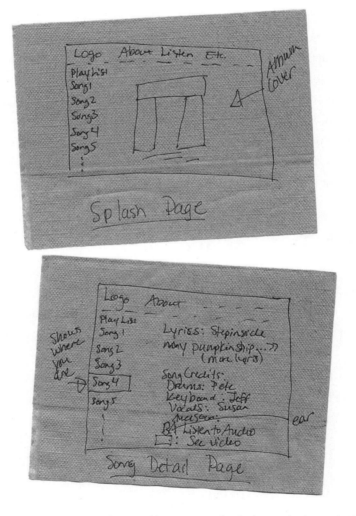

3.1   As soon as you put pen to bar napkins, you can begin to conduct user testing. You can save time and money by letting potential users find problems with your interface ideas. The earlier you have groups of two, three, or six respond to your work, the fewer resources you will eventually have to throw at correcting problems.

In 2000, when I was working for The Branch Libraries of The New York Public Library, we hired Small Company (www.smallco.net) to move our printed events calendar to the web. Before he spent any time on planning or production, Albert Harum-Alvares, the founder of Small Company, visited a few of our branch libraries to meet and talk with some of our users.

He used a printed version of the calendar as a jumping-off point for these conversations. At this early stage, it was not the interface he was interested in discussing, but the calendar's data and how it would be used.

Albert sat at a small table in the Epiphany Branch of The New York Public Library on East 23rd Street for an entire afternoon, talking to members of our four target audiences: children, teens, adults, and adults with small children.

He asked them questions such as these:

□ How far are you willing to travel to participate in an event?

□ What is the most important consideration for you in selecting an event?

□ Do you normally schedule events in advance, or do you attend them spontaneously?

We learned some important things from our users. Teenagers, perhaps the least fettered members of our audience, were willing to travel far and were interested in seeing event listings in all Boroughs. Adults with small children, on the other hand, were only willing to travel to branches in their immediate region and had small windows of free time to spend on events. Our interface would have to accommodate these different user needs.

These results surprised us: We had expected our users to have similar needs. The variation across age groups was implemented into our design, allowing us to better serve our users.

The cost of this preliminary user testing was low; we had to pay for only a few hours of Albert's time. The benefit was that, at the outset of the project, we had corrected several false assumptions about our users (see Figure 3.2).

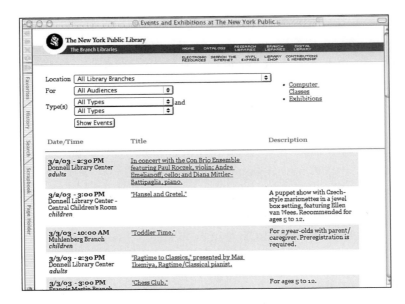

3.2 *Before we began production for this events calendar, our web-development consultant spent a few hours in one of our branch libraries talking to members of our audience about how they used our printed events calendar.*

Spinning Straw into Gold

By conducting this economical and informal study early, we corrected important assumptions about our users' needs and fixed several organizational problems. You can avoid the expense of fixing interface problems while you are in production if you conduct small-scale preproduction user tests.

Lather, Rinse, Repeat

Here is good news for your budget: You do not need to test more than 6–12 users. After interviewing that number of people, you will reach a point of diminishing returns. In his wonderful book *Don't Make Me Think!* (Que, 2000), Steve Krug offers the following advice: "If you really want to know if your web site works, ask your next-door neighbor to try using it, while you watch. (You bring the beer.)"

Even asking three friends or colleagues to do a 15-minute test can help you catch interface problems. Conduct tests often. Each time you reach a significant development milestone, conduct a test that consists of tasks, as described in the next section.

A Simple User Study

Gather a small group of test users. Again, five or six is a good number, but even two or three will tell you much of what you need to know. Do not worry about who the test users are; just make sure that they are not your colleagues who are also working on your project.

Conduct your test with a partner. One of you should talk to the users; the other should take notes. If you each have a copy of the list of tasks, one of you can use that list to take notes from.

Invite your users to sit at an office computer. Thank them for their time. Tell the users that they are looking at an early version of your site and that you would like them to try to use the site to accomplish a few tasks. Make sure they know that if they run into trouble, the site is at fault, not them. You do this to be certain that they are comfortable, will answer honestly, and will not be made to feel stupid. (When people feel stupid, they tend to clam up.)

Ask users to perform specific, real-world tasks. For instance, if you are working on an e-commerce site, you might ask users to find a particular item, add it to their shopping cart, and then buy it. If the site is a searchable gallery of images, try asking your users to find and bookmark a specific image. (This will help you discover whether your metadata is working and your search engine is doing what it should.) The number and duration of tasks should be short; a 15-minute session will be plenty.

Ask your test subjects to accomplish each task one at a time. Here is the most important part: Ask them to think out loud. As they articulate their assumptions and problems, have your record-keeping partner jot down notes on what is said. If a particular task looks like it will be impossible, thank the test user and ask him to move on to the next task.

Prepare a parting gift for your user: a gift certificate, a small chunk of cash, or whatever else you can afford. Your usability test subjects have generously donated their time, and you had better give them something in return.

After you and your partners have gone through the data, make whatever adjustments are necessary to your site. Again, if you are conducting tests on a regular basis, these adjustments should be relatively minor and not too costly.

Shoestring Usability Toolkit

All through high school and college, I waited tables—and I must tell you that I was not good at it. I was not only slow and disorganized, but I interfered in the dining experience. I was a fussy, oppressive presence that distracted from the pleasure of the food and company that was supposed to be the focus of the restaurant-goer's user experience.

I would like to think that I am a better web professional than I was a waitress. But being a bad waitress taught me a valuable lesson about creating usable customer experiences: Customers want to enjoy the experience, not think about it. As a web professional, I work hard to create interfaces that serve the user without calling undue attention to themselves.

When users have to think about the interface, or the waitress, something is not working. A good interface, like a good waitress, is invisible. I don't care whether you are working in Joe's Diner or at The Four Seasons; your customer should never have to give your service enough thought to evaluate it.

It takes a long time to learn how to become a good waitress, and it takes a similar investment to become a good interface designer. Creating usable web sites does not come intuitively to all web professionals. If you are working on a shoestring project, if you have no extra money for usability experts, and if usability is not your area of expertise, you will have to learn to make do.

To help you become an instant expert, I offer a few guidelines. I only wish that I had been given such tips when I started waiting tables. (Ba-dump-bum!)

Guidelines for Menus and Navigation

The first thing to know about web site usability is that there are no rules for presentation, but there are important guidelines. Here are a few of my favorites.

Keep a Light Burning in the Window

Not all users will enter your site from your home page. Some will arrive at internal pages via search engines. Make sure that you have your logo, theme line, and site navigation on every page so that these back-door users can find their way around as easily as if they had come through the front door.

Economic Click Counts

The three-click rule is a good guideline for site navigation. Many usability experts will tell you that users should not have to click more than three times to find what they are looking for. For example, a user might click from the home page of a shopping site to the Women's section, from Women's to Shoes, and from Women's Shoes to a particular style of shoe. This three-click rule is a useful general guideline, but what is probably more important than the number of clicks is how easy each link is to find. Steve Krug offers this insight in *Don't Make Me Think*: If your navigation is intuitive and provides good feedback, and if the path from general to specific information makes sense, users will forgive the number of clicks.

Warm and Straightforward Language

We dive into writing for the web in the next chapter, but in the meantime, know that copy for this medium works best when it is honest, warm, and straightforward. Web users have a low tolerance for marketing jargon and insincere dribble.

The Rule of Five

The final guideline that I'll leave you with is the rule of five, which advises site crafters to keep menus five items long or less. The thinking behind this guideline is simple: Users often glaze over when they are faced with endless lists. "Too many choices" feels like no choice at all. There are many exceptions to this rule. eBay.com, for example, has no trouble getting users to wade through long lists. But eBay users are highly motivated. Unless you are selling $200 Sony Aibo dogs, you should probably stick to the rule of five.

Recyclable HTML Library

Late in the winter of 2003, New York City had a record snowfall. A colleague slipped on her way to work and fractured her right arm. A day or two after the break, we were on the phone trying to schedule a lunch date. "Here is where I find out if I can still use my calendar software," she muttered. With her right arm out of commission, she could not use her mouse and had to depend instead on her keyboard to navigate her third-party web-based calendar. The task was difficult. Some of the screen areas that she needed to navigate to were hard to reach by hitting the tab key on her keyboard. Unfortunately for my colleague, the calendar's web interface was not designed to have a logical tab order, so she had to punch her way through long lists of menu items before she could click on the tool to schedule a new appointment.

> ### Spinning Straw into Gold
>
> The way you write your HTML can have a large impact on the usability of your site. Bloated markup makes pages slow to download. Badly written HTML forms are frustrating to use. These kinds of problems are easily and affordably corrected with good markup. Paying careful attention to the way you author HTML will result in a tremendous return on the time invested, giving you more control over the user experience that you are creating. We cover more economic advantages to writing good markup in Chapter 7, "Save Time and Money with Web Standards."

The HTML behind the intranet calendar site lacked polish and was thus difficult for my colleague to use. Such polish is expensive, but web site usability depends heavily on good markup. If you invest time in creating a recyclable HTML library that includes features such as tab order indexing (described in detail later), you can reuse that markup, thus lowering your costs over time and providing a nice return on investment for your efforts.

Markup, Usability, and Web Site Accessibility

Building a good HTML library does more than just make your site easy to use for the majority of your public. It also makes your site more accessible to users with disabilities.

Web professionals often work with clients who think that they can't afford to build accessible web sites. It is true that it can cost more to make a site accessible. For one thing, you have to work harder to make a site properly serve users with disabilities, and your time is money. But there are five economic advantages to making accessibility a priority early in the game:

1. Accessibility helps not only users with permanent disabilities such as blindness and mobility impairments, but also those with temporary disabilities, as with my colleague who fell on the ice. Why build a site that alienates users?

2. Accessibility makes your site easier to use for nontraditional receiving devices such as PalmPilots and web-enabled mobile phones. We go into an affordable way to design for nontraditional devices in Chapter 7.

3. Some site owners can face lawsuits if they don't make their sites accessible, and we all know how expensive litigation is.

4. It is far less expensive to make your site accessible if you start at the beginning, but if you have to retro-fit an existing site into accessibility, the cost can be dear. Making accessibility a requirement of a new site adds about 3% to your budget, while retrofitting an existing site into accessibility can cost much, much more than that. For instance, on a handspun shoestring site that is built without the benefit of a content-management system, it might take a few extra minutes per page to specify tab order or provide alternative functionality for those who cannot use JavaScript (explained a bit later in this chapter). But the time and cost involved in this change of daily work habits is nothing compared to that of an entire site restructuring. Changing your work habits now is like saving your pennies for a rainy day.

5. Some sites are legally obligated to be accessible to users with disabilities. Section 508 of the U.S. Rehabilitation Act requires federal agencies to make their electronic and information technology accessible to people with disabilities. It is not yet clear how broadly this amendment applies. If you are working on a .gov site, or if your .edu or .org is funded by a federal source, you might need to worry about Section 508. Other national and state governments are beginning to ask the same of certain kinds of web sites.

Budget Threat: Accessibility

If you suspect that you will have to make your site accessible to disabled users some day in the future and you think that you can save money by putting that concern on the back burner, think again. It costs an extra 3% to make a site accessible if you incorporate accessibility into the design and production from the get-go. However, if you try to retrofit a site into accessibility compliance, it will cost many times that. Do your bank account a favor and make accessibility a priority from day one.

The following markup suggestions will help you create a web site that is usable for the broadest possible audience. If you have never paid careful attention to HTML, it might take you awhile before you stop feeling like this is slowing you down. Hang in there. You'll soon master this new way of working, and you will become more efficient and more in control of your work than you imagined was possible. You will also see a return on this investment of time in the form of more users and fewer complaints.

Tab Order

Let's return to my colleague whose temporary injury left her unable to use her web-based calendar. Tab order is a vital usability feature that many developers often overlook.

Try this test: Unplug your mouse from your computer for one afternoon, and try to navigate the web only by tabbing your keyboard. You'll quickly see how difficult it is—and also realize how easy it *should* be. Tabbing through a site should take a web user through the pages easily and efficiently. The user should be able to skip navigation when needed. The user also should be able to tab to key content areas easily, skipping from feature areas as logically and quickly as they can be visually scanned.

Take a look at Figure 3.3, which shows one of my email accounts. If I wanted to tab through this page, I would have to tab through every mailbox in the left side and then tab through all of the top navigation before I could tab to the messages in my inbox. Think of my colleague who temporarily lost the use of her right arm. Think about people who can never use a mouse! A site like this email application would be incredibly time-consuming and frustrating to use. You don't create web sites to hurt people (even inadvertently); you create them to help people.

There is an easy way to fix the tab order problem: Define tab order in advance. Take a look at Figure 3.3 and the code that follows it. Both show the markup for the email site, but the second chunk of code shows a predefined tab order.

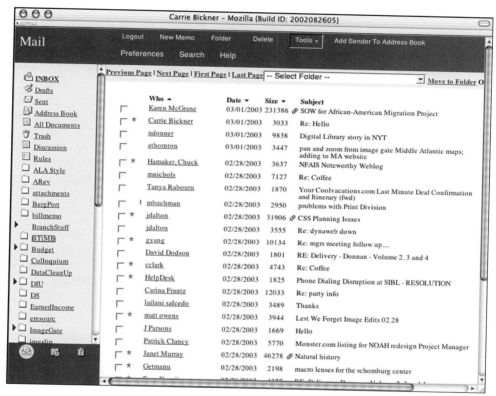

3.3 *Accessibility woes are actually a specific form of usability problem. This image shows an email program with a tab order that is less than ideal: Navigating to new messages requires the user to tediously tab through each of the menu items on the top and left navigation. This is a problem that is easily solved by prescribing a tab order.*

```
<table>
<tr>
<td><input type="checkbox" name="somename" value="001" /></td>
<td><a href="openmail.html">Carrie Bickner</a></td>
<td>03/01/2003</td><td>231386</td><td>SOW Migration Project</td>
</tr>
```

To access the first message in the email pictured in Figure 3.3, the user must tab through the left navigation before arriving at the first message in the inbox.

```
<table>
<tr>
<td><input type="checkbox" name="somename" value="001" tabindex="1" /></td>
<td><a href="openmail.html" tabindex="2">Carrie Bickner</a></td>
<td>03/01/2003</td><td>231386</td><td>SOW for Migration Project</td>
</tr>
```

The tab problem is easily fixed by adding a `tabindex` attribute to the form element or link that you want users to start with. A link with the `tabindex="1"` attribute is the first link that a user tabs to. When this `tabindex` attribute is part of your recyclable HTML library, you'll find yourself using it in all of your work. As these and other good markup habits become part of your repertoire, you will see the cost of producing more polished, usable HTML go down.

Forms

Here's a paradox for you: It is surprisingly *easy* to make forms *hard to use* for anyone who can't use a mouse. Take a look at the form in Figure 3.4. The absence of a Submit button makes this item unnecessarily difficult to use for anyone keyboarding through the site. As soon as you tab to the menu and start to arrow down the flavors, the form begins to process after you cursor through the first option. Essentially, Chocolate is the only option available to people who cannot use a mouse. If you wanted to select Lemon, you would need to use a mouse. Adding a Submit button would solve the problem without requiring much extra work. This easy markup nuance provides a quick way to make your site more usable to a broad group of people (see Figure 3.5).

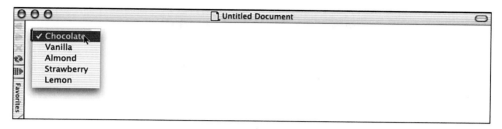

3.4 *A menu without a Submit button is like a door without a knob if you can't use a mouse. After you cursor to the first menu item—in this case, Chocolate—the form is processed. Keyboard users do not have a chance to select another flavor, to select multiple flavors, or to rethink their options. Bad accessibility equals bad usability.*

3.5 *Adding a Submit button to the form makes it usable to people who navigate your site without a mouse. They will be able to move up and down the selection list, and they will have a better experience, equivalent to that of mouse users.*

JavaScript

As you add to your library, take into consideration that some of your users will not have JavaScript. Some (surprisingly, about 10%) use a JavaScript-capable browser but turn off JavaScript because of exaggerated security fears. Others use devices that do not support JavaScript. Considering these users' needs is especially important when designing navigational elements that use JavaScript. Sometimes navigation options are not even visible until the user mouses over an area; when the mouse is placed over a hot spot, a menu appears. This might be fun for the JavaScript-capable, but it makes the site useless to other people. Include the same navigation options without JavaScript, perhaps by placing a text menu elsewhere on the page. Better still, make that text menu more accessible by using a `tabindex` attribute that directs the visitor who is not using a mouse to the first item on that menu.

It is also a friendly idea to make redundant calls to JavaScript functions for all mouseover events, as shown in the following markup example. When you spend that afternoon browsing the web without a mouse, you will see how important this easy work is.

```
<a href="thepage.html" onmouseout="swapImgRestore()"
onblur="swapImgRestore()" onmouseover="swapImage('Image1','','susan2.gif',1)"
onfocus="swapImage('Image1','','susan2.gif',1)"><img src="susan.gif"
name="Image1" width="200" height="200" alt="Susan" /></a>
```

These two sets of JavaScript events create the rollover. One set comprises the onmouseout *and* onmouseover *conditions. This set is simple enough: When the user mouses over, the image susan.gif is replaced by susan2.gif. When the user mouses away, the* onmouseout *condition causes the original susan.gif image to reappear. But what about site visitors who are not using a mouse? How can they enjoy the rollover effect? The redundant* onfocus *and* onblur *events take care of that. If a visitor tabs to the image, the* onfocus *event is triggered and that visitor enjoys the same rollover effect as a mouse user. The* onblur *event is triggered when the visitor tabs away.*

Expanding Your HTML Library

With each project that you work on, you will have more goodies to add to your HTML library and more opportunities to take advantage of the resources that you are building for yourself. As a shoestring web professional, you will use these resources repeatedly, lowering the production cost of each site you create. Developing these materials will take time, but if you are careful about the markup that you create, you can leverage that work in the future. In Chapter 7, we go over more techniques that will help make you a better, more efficient web professional.

Chapter 4

Why Good Copy Counts

Chapter Checklist

1. **Words matter more when you have few resources.**

   The language of your site is the element that you have the most control over, and it requires little in the way of technological or financial expenditures.

2. **Good copy can elevate a low-budget site.**

   If you do not have a big budget for design, the copy can become the hero of your site. Clean, straightforward, well-written language can elevate the site by giving it a mood and tone that is appropriate to your product. This can be as powerful as—and perhaps even more powerful than—the work you do on the visual design.

3. **Write in a way that is honest and straightforward.**

   When people read on the web, they have less patience with copy and are slightly more skeptical than they are with other media. Avoid hyperbolic statements and marketing talk. This style might work in print, but it is off-putting on the web. Keep your ideas on target, and tell users what they need to know.

4. **Keep it simple but not simplistic.**

   Again, dare to do less. Use language that is simple and straightforward. Keep sentences short and to the point. Do not, however, dumb down your content, which will make your company look silly and insult your users. Remember, too, that the shorter the copy is, the less expensive it will be to edit.

5. **Avoid spelling and grammatical errors.**

   Nothing undermines a beautifully constructed site like spelling and grammatical errors. Allocate resources to allow for a full copy edit on all new content.

6. **Free real estate.**

   Take advantage of free real estate and the power that only words can deliver: Use title tags, email signature files, error messages, and other content areas to your advantage.

❝ ❝ *Clever words are not as good as straight talk.* ❞ ❞

—Chinese proverb

Words are the low-tech, platform-independent, inexpensive glue that hold a site together. When used well, words compel users to make purchases, lead people from an email newsletter to your site, entice users to stay on your site, and even keep them on your site when they come upon well-crafted error messages. Words distinguish your site from your competitors' and let your visitors know that a human rather than merely software is behind your web presence.

Words are the only aspect of a site that you have complete control over. The display of graphic design always depends on the user's receiving device, whether that is a handheld device, a voice browser, or a plain old web browser whose display settings might customize away your design. You have no control over your users' preferences for plug-ins, typographical display, or any other presentation options. Words, however, display in the exact same sequence that you type them.

Words have the power not only to shape your site's literal message, but also to tell the user who you are and what you care about simply through the voice they establish. When words are used ineptly, your site might ring of apathy, empty bravado, or anonymity. If the language of your site is full of spelling and grammatical problems, words can give the user the impression that you have weak attention to detail, that you might not know what you are talking about, and that you are not that smart. When used well, however, words can infuse your site with a sense of smarts, warmth, concern, humor, or whatever else you want to convey.

The wise shoestring designer pays careful attention to a site's copy and directs significant resources to writing and editing. This does not mean that your copy needs to be a literary masterpiece, nor does it mean that you have to hire an expensive copywriter for your site—although if you can, do so. Careful attention to copy does mean that you must dedicate a good portion of your production time to writing, editing, and copy editing, and that the text on your site must be genuine, human, and to the point.

This chapter is for web professionals who are responsible for many aspects of web production and who probably can't afford to hire the recommended writer and editor.

What Is Good Writing?

Nick Usborne, author of *Net Words* and the expert who I consulted while writing this chapter, left me with the perfect way of describing good copy and what it can do for a low-budget web site:

"When you write well, everything else takes care of itself. Good writing is always simple. Good writing is clear. It is honest. It is free of hyperbole. It is free of drama, exclamation points, and excessive bolding of the text. If you feel that your sentence needs special emphasis, write a better sentence; don't dress it up with bold words and extra colors.

"Can good writing elevate a potentially 'cheap' site? Absolutely. The core value of the site is found in the quality of the writing. Good writing can elevate anything! But then, I am a little biased—correct, but biased."

What Makes Good Web Copy?

Writing well for the web does not mean that you have to be the most skilled or high-paid writer around. We are not trying to give our users a literary experience; we are trying to get them what they need. To do this, use language that is:

1. Honest and straightforward.
2. Broken up in short, concise chunks and peppered with meaningful blurbs and headlines.
3. About the user, not you.
4. Simple, but not simplistic.
5. Free of spelling and grammatical errors.
6. Rotated on a regular basis.

When you think of these six characteristics of good web copy, think about all the places on a site where you use words:

- Body copy
- Callouts and highlights
- Headers
- Title tags
- Navigation
- Error messages

At every place where text appears, the shoestring web professional takes advantage of the power of the written word and uses the principles of good web copy to maximize that power.

Budget Threat

Nothing can undermine the success of your site as easily as bad copy. Users have no tolerance for insincere jargon, and they lose confidence in a site riddled with bad grammar. If you have taken the time and money to create a beautiful design or to develop powerful software, do not undermine those investments by neglecting to take good care of the content.

Be Honest and Straightforward

Returning to the sage insight of Nick Usborne, we know that when people read on the web, they are much more skeptical than when they read a book, a brochure, a newspaper, or any other printed material. Usborne maintains that the same hyperbole that people tolerate in print puts them off when they encounter it on the web. The glib language of marketing will fail you if you use it on the web.

I add to that idea that even the happiest web user is just a click away from the frustration of conducting business on the web. Taking these ideas together, most visitors are a pretty prickly bunch, and the web professional's job is to keep them from feeling skeptical and frustrated. The best and easiest way to do this is to keep your words honest and to the point—simply tell your users what they need to know.

Take a look at Figures 4.1 and 4.2. Figure 4.1 is the Swimmers Guide site as I found it. Notice the theme line—the descriptive text "More information about more swimming pools in more places than on any other resource! More swimming links than any of the swimming indexes!." What does this text tell the reader about what the site does?

Spinning Straw into Gold

Far too often, good copy is buried deep in a site's internal pages, while hyperbolic language floats to the top. Take advantage of the stronger language by promoting it to the splash page.

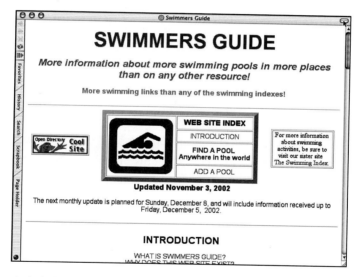

4.1 *Hyperbole helps no one. The theme line—or lines, really—in the Swimmers Guide (www.swimmersguide.com/) is hyperbolic drivel. It does not even tell us whether the site is about public pools, building pools, pools for purchase, or pools of the rich and famous. Who cares that the site offers the most information about swimming pools? We want to know what kind of information is there and how good it is. Tell us more of what we need to know.*

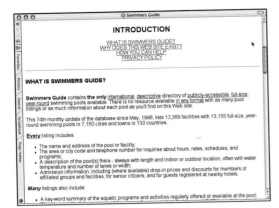

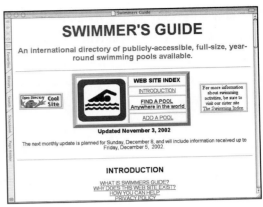

4.2 *Tell us who you are and what your site does. Using some copy that was squirreled away on an About page (left), I edited the theme line for this revised version of the site (right). Now we know what the site does. You can make something from nothing by moving your best copy to the home page.*

Now read the copy as I have edited it in Figure 4.2: "An international directory of publicly-accessible, full-size, year-round swimming pools available." This is copy that I found buried down a level in the site. So often the most engaging and descriptive language is buried on a site as an afterthought. This probably is because when people are not trying as hard, the real idea of what they are trying to sell comes to the surface in a human voice. Think about the copy that you have already written, languishing in the corners of your site. If you have good copy like this—copy that tells what your site does—bring it out. It is no more expensive to use your best copy up front on your splash page than it is to bury it.

The hyperbolic theme line in Figure 4.1 might do well in the Yellow Pages, but when you have a potentially impatient audience of web users, give them the straight dope. Keep it honest and straightforward; tell them exactly what they need to know. The Hendersonville County Public Library site is a fine example of this, shown in Figure 4.3. At the very top of the site is the telephone number for the director of that library. In highlighting the phone number of the person in charge, this site delivers in a straightforward way information that is probably in high demand among that library's audience.

4.3 *Relevant copy can be as simple as a phone number.*

Cutting to the chase with web copy will not cost more than droning on will. You do not need special software or hardware. Shorter copy also means that you have fewer words to edit. If you pay by the word for copy or copy editing, striving for short, to-the-point text will reduce content costs. It also means that you can get more material above the fold, giving the user a better idea of what else the site offers, and giving you a better return on your writing investment.

Break Text into Small Chunks and Use Headlines Liberally

In a May 2002 eye-tracking study conducted by Stanford University and The Poynter Institute (www.wired.com/news/culture/0,1284,36104,00.html), researchers found that on news sites, users scan headlines and blurbs before zeroing in on content that they then read word for word. It is safe to extrapolate beyond the newspaper web site genre and apply this insight to other kinds of web sites, such as school and library sites, church and community sites, and small business sites. The lesson is obvious: Chunk text into bite-size pieces, and give your users headlines and blurbs to read, as shown in Figure 4.4.

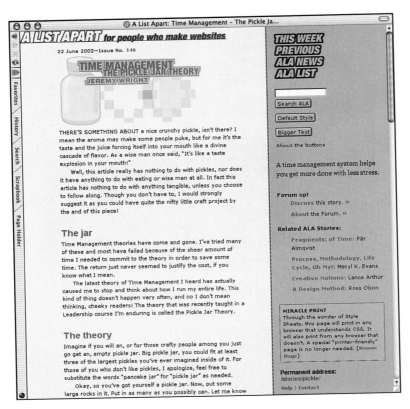

4.4 *A List Apart (*`www.alistapart.com/`*) is a weekly magazine for people who make web sites. As a not-for-profit, ALA operates on a budget that is practically nonexistent. Each article is chunked into small, bite-size paragraphs and is broken into manageable intellectual pieces with meaningful headlines. If your site has long pieces of content, be sure to chunk text in this way and to write straightforward, meaningful headlines. The headlines will help users.*

When we learned to write in school, our language teachers drilled into our heads that paragraphs are buckets for related thoughts. We were taught to create a new paragraph only when we had a new idea. Ignore this well-learned rule when you write for the web, or learn to define "new idea" somewhat more liberally. Remember that reading on the computer screen sucks and that your site visitors need visual relief if they are going to read anything on your site at all.

We have been emphasizing the notion of "daring to do less" as an important theme for any successful shoestring web site; here the idea might be applied to the length of copy. Write shorter paragraphs, and this should alleviate the need to chunk text randomly.

Also remember that you can craft condensed versions of an idea and then use hypertext to link to a more detailed version of the same topic.

Breaking text into small chunks is not quite enough. It is also important that you give your readers headlines and subheads to help them navigate though passages. This not only helps them scan and digest content, but it also helps them keep track of where they are as they scroll through longer pages.

The irony of this low-tech chunking and headline technique is that it does a presentation job that more involved and expensive design work can't do nearly so easily: It makes text look good on the page.

Write About the User, Not About You

If I had a nickel for every site that seemed to be having a conversation with itself, I would be a wealthy woman. The tendency to use words in a self-absorbed rather than user-centered manner comes out in profound ways. Some of the best examples are in site navigation.

Figure 4.5 shows a site for a continuing education program at the University of Connecticut. Turn your attention to the first item on the left navigation pane. Centers and Institutes seems innocuous enough, but think about the analogous link in the UCLA continuing education site (see Figure 4.6); Fields of Study is less about the structure of the school and more about the options available to the student.

Each school offers a travel-study program. On the University of Connecticut site, the link to this program is labeled International Studies; this is a description of the program. The link to the travel-study program at UCLA is in the spotlight area in the middle of the page; the text for this program describes the student's experience. UCLA takes the user-centered language principle one step further by personalizing the copy and giving a short blurb about one student's experience.

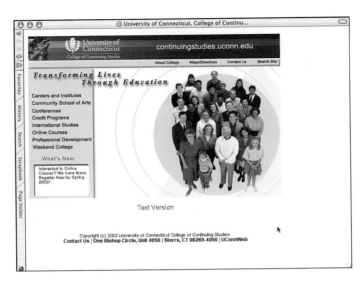

4.5 *The copy in the University of Connecticut Continuing Education program site is about the program (http://continuingstudies.uconn.edu/). Even the theme line, "Transforming Lives Through Education," is about the program, not about the students. It is a hard habit to break, but try to write about the user rather than about your program.*

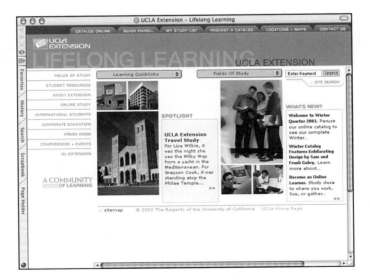

4.6 *The University of Southern California also has a Continuing Education Program (www.uclaextension.org). The language in this site is more about the student and less about the program. The theme line, "Lifelong Learning," is about the process or experience of the student, not about the program.*

One last comparison, and then I'll give the University of Connecticut a break. Each school offers online courses. The University of Connecticut labels the link to this section of the site with the left menu item, Online Courses. UCLA takes us to the same information with the label Become an Online Learner at the bottom right of the page.

Using language that is about the user rather than your site does not cost you any extra money, and it adds warmth and humanity to your site that can come from nowhere else.

My Whatever

Don't try to personalize content that is not personal. It is just silly. For a time, *The New York Times* on the web got caught up in the "My Whatever" label; we saw sections called My Finance and My Real Estate. When I go to the *Times*, however, I am not looking for information about my finances. I already have that information. I am looking for financial information about New York City, the United States, and the world. There is nothing personal about what I am looking for.

From a writing standpoint, the "My Whatever" label is a bad move strategically, especially when you are writing site navigation. If most or all of your navigation labels begin with the word *My*, they are more difficult to read quickly. Which of the following two lists is easier to scan?

My Finance	Finance
My Style	Style
My Real Estate	Real Estate
My Catalog	Catalog

Personalization *functions* make sense on certain web sites: I happen to like news sites that let me customize the screen so that articles about science appear before articles about sports. I am not suggesting that we do away with personalization features; this is simply a warning about getting wonky with overly personalized language.

Keep It Simple but Not Simplistic

Make sure that your sentences are short and to the point. Try to avoid compound sentences, especially as you introduce products and services. Figure 4.7 shows a fabulous no-no from the United States Post Office (`www.usps.com/zip4/`).

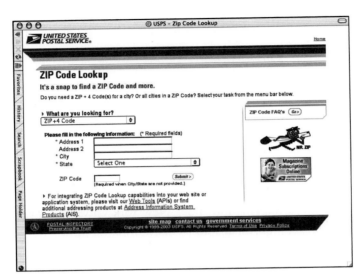

4.7   *Most of the copy on this ZIP code lookup page (`www.usps.com`) is just fine. The text "Do you need a ZIP + 4 code(s) for a city? Or all cities in a ZIP code?" is straightforward and tells the user what she or he can do with this page. But take a look at what follows it.*

The following copy looks like it was written by a programmer when the site was still in beta:

> For integrating ZIP code lookup capabilities into your web site or application system, please visit our web tools (APIs) or find additional addressing products at Address Information System Products (AIS).

This is not to slam programmers; something happens to the brain while one is engaged in application development that makes it very hard to write for humans. I have seen it happen to the most articulate people. If you are the person doing both the programming and the writing, make sure you give yourself time to clean up the copy in post-production. A simple turn of phrase such as the following might do the trick:

Add ZIP code lookup to your web site. See our other address system products.

Well-intended writers sometimes think that web copy needs to be chatty, even glib. Not so. In fact, such an approach can be a bit embarrassing.

Consider the IRS web site shown in Figure 4.8 as a warning (`http://www.irs.gov/individuals/`):

Where's My Refund?

Get the lowdown on your refund now. Secure access anytime from anywhere. What a deal!

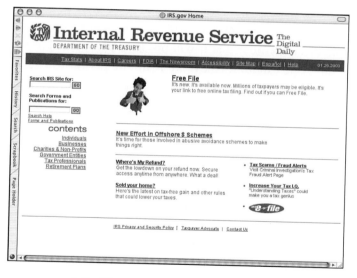

4.8 *What a deal indeed (`www.irs.gov`).*
How does "get the lowdown" help me find refund information?

Remember also that the voice you use needs to reflect the company or organization that you are writing for. I know that the IRS is trying to be a more friendly and accessible agency, but we are never going to want to get down with them, and this inappropriate voice is a bit jarring. Who are we trying to kid? Why waste words on chatty copy that feels awkward and offers no real value to your customers?

I might rewrite IRS copy thusly and save the slang for when I am hanging with my peeps:

Where's My Refund?

Check the status of your refund online now.

Keep Your Site Free of Spelling and Grammatical Errors

The best way to undermine your user's confidence in your product and your message is to publish a site that is riddled with spelling and grammatical errors. Use your spell checker, but remember that it will not help you with all errors. Take the time to review your copy carefully. Ask more than one person to check your text. Just as with shoestring usability, described in the previous chapter, shoestring copy editing and proofreading does not require the services of expensive professionals (although, if you can afford those professionals, it's money well spent). Shoestring copy editing and proofreading relies on the fact that two heads are better than one and that one pair of eyes can catch what another misses. Ask a colleague to look over your work before taking it live.

Keep an eye open for common language misuses. Know the difference between *it's* and *its, your* and *you're,* and *affect* and *effect.*

I am not the best at spelling, nor am I especially adept at distinguishing between homonyms. Every time I use the word *palette,* I have to check the dictionary to see that I should not be using *palate.* I know more than anyone how long it takes to thoroughly check language, spelling, and grammar, but as one who has suffered the embarrassment of these errors, I understand the value of good copy editing. If you do not have this kind of talent on your staff, make sure to find a way to have your site copy edited.

At one time in our history, grammar and spelling were taught more rigorously than they are now. You might be able to find a product of this old-school education who can do copy editing for you at shoestring rates. Check local community organizations that cater to the gray–hair set. You might also be able to find a poor college or graduate student in your area who will be happy to be paid by the word.

If you simply can't afford a copy editor, or even if you can, take this advice: Read *The Elements of Style*, by William Strunk Jr., E. B. White, and Roger Angell. The book is now in its fourth edition. I promise that this will be the best $8 you ever spend. This book will save you from looking stupid by pointing out the most common grammatical and word choice errors that we are all prone to making.

Free and Inexpensive Real Estate

Now that you have a handle on what makes good web copy, let's think about where copy goes. There is so much more to writing for the web than the copy that goes into your site navigation and body.

Title Tag

The `<title>` tag is the element that usually displays in the top chrome of the browser window and declares, obviously, the title of your page (see Figure 4.9). (I'll talk about where this element fits structurally in an HTML document in Chapter 7, "Save Time and Money with Web Standards.") The title element is among the first several lines of markup in the HTML, and it looks like this:

```
<title>The Rogue Librarian -- Shooshin' and stampin' </title>
```

The content of your `<title>` element displays in some very valuable places: in search engine results (see Figure 4.10), in the browser's title bar (see Figure 4.11), and in the browser's bookmarks. The title element might also be used in web applications such as newsfeeds and "email to a friend" applications. Thus, making good use of this element is vital when it is presented outside the context of your own site. The small pieces of screen real estate have a value that is surprisingly high, like the rent on a shoebox apartment in Manhattan. Use it, by gum, and use it well.

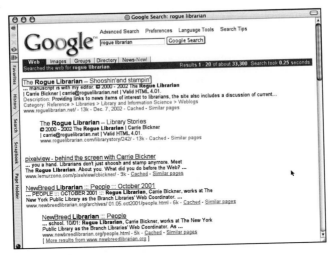

4.9 *The text that you write for the* `<title>` *tag appears in search engine results (*`www.google.com`*). This is true for many web search engines and also for internal site search engines. This screen shot illustrates what happens if you do not take the time to write a* `<title>` *element for each page; you give the user little opportunity to distinguish your site's sections from one another.*

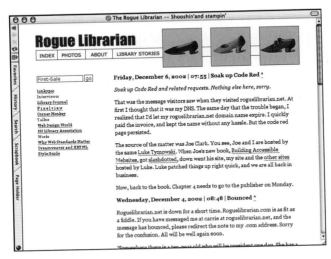

4.10 *The contents of the* `<title>` *element display in the title bar of most browsers, letting your users see where they are (*`www.roguelibrarian.com`*). Think about the value of this information to users who like to multitask and have several browser windows open at one time. Be descriptive when you write this copy. Some browser windows cut the title short. Try to keep the character count to less than 45. As mentioned earlier in this chapter, it is best to be concise. Use words economically.*

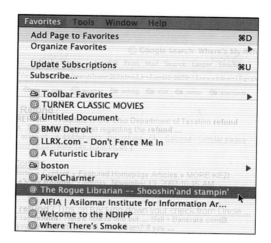

4.11 *Another place where the* <title> *tag appears is in bookmarks.
If you hope that users will bookmark more than one page from your site, make sure
that each page has its own descriptive* <title>. *You can include your company name,
but augment that information with descriptive copy.*

The <title> element is neglected in several ways. Occasionally, it is left unused altogether. Sometimes the title of the site is the <title> element that appears on every page within that site. When this happens, it is difficult for users to tell the difference between parts of your site when they come upon them in their bookmarks and in search engine results. If you have invested time and money in an internal search engine for your site, and you have failed to write meaningful title elements for each page or section of your site, you are selling that search engine investment short. If you run a small online retail store and your users are looking for shoes, *Company Name: Shoes* makes a better title element for the shoes page than unadorned *Company Name*.

Look again at Figure 4.9, where you see a Google search result for my personal site, Rogue Librarian. The first two search results are for different parts of my site, and the title tag for each is different. The home page has my title and theme line, and the subsection called "Library Stories" has a title appropriate to that section. Be sure to use title tags that are as descriptive as possible for each section of your site.

Links

The most important characteristic of the web is that it is a system of hyperlinks. A *hyperlink* is an element in a web page or site that links or points to another place in that same page or to a different page or site. Although you can create hyperlinks around and within images, the most effective hyperlinks are built around text.

Good web writers are careful about the words they use to create a hyperlink. Consider these three examples:

<u>My mother</u> told me that chocolate is essential for women's health.

My mother told me that <u>chocolate</u> is essential for women's health.

My mother told that chocolate is essential for <u>women's health</u>.

The placement of each link raises different expectations about what the user is going to find—not only the subject, but how users might be predisposed to understand what they find. The link in the first example probably leads to a page on which my mother is the subject. The audience might be predisposed to taking what my mother says with a grain of salt. Obviously, in the second example, chocolate is the subject, and we are predisposed to think that this link will take us to enjoyable information, such as a recipe for a killer chocolate cake. The third example raises the expectation that *The New England Journal of Medicine* has just published an article that declares that chocolate is good for women, thus vindicating my mother's long-held but suspect belief that I should eat chocolate every day.

Paying careful attention to where you place links will not cost much money—and if you are smart about it, you can let language do much of the heavy lifting for the navigational issues on your site.

The title Attribute

Selecting a good piece of text is not the only way you can exploit the power of words. You can do one other quick and easy thing to add tremendous value to your site: Write a `title` attribute. The `title` attribute can be used in the hyperlink to provide more information about the link.

The `title` attribute in this example lets the user know that the link points to a study about chocolate and information on how it is good for women's health. The text in the `title` attribute displays as a ToolTip in most browsers (see Figure 4.12):

```
<p>My mother told me that chocolate is essential for
<a href="http://www.somesciencejournal.com"
title="New study finds chocolate is high in iron.">women's health</a>.</p>
```

Taking the time to write well-crafted `title` attributes can add more information to your site. This can be a place to add copy that is too long to include on the page but that might be valuable to your readers, or that can supply more guidance to other pages on your site. At the cost of a minute's additional work, `title` attributes enhance user experience and increase the perceived value of the information your site provides.

4.12 The text "New study finds chocolate is high in iron." is a `title` attribute in the anchor link tag that displays as the user mouses over the link (www.somesciencejournal.com). Use the `title` attribute to provide extra information. Note that not all browsers support the `title` attribute. Those of us who still have to worry about Netscape 4 should know that that ancient browser does not support the `title` attribute; Netscape 4 users will never see this text.

Email Signatures

If you are not using a signature file in your email, start now (see Figure 4.13). Most email clients enable you to create this bit of text that is automatically appended to every message you send. This is free marketing and an opportunity to have fun. If your company has a theme line, use it. Include your URL. If you have something new to promote on your site, write a short blurb that goes out with every message you send. Do it—it is free! Be careful that you do not overdo it, though.

Remember that people reading your mail will not tolerate verbose signatures. A good rule of thumb is to keep your signature at less than four lines; just make those four lines count. The shorter you write, the more power you grant each word—and the likelier your message is to be read by busy Internet users, who have no time for long texts.

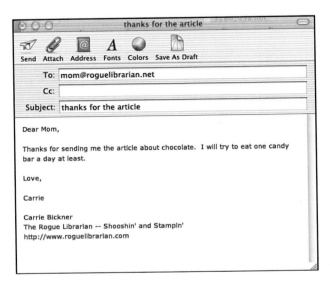

4.13 *Email signatures are free marketing. In my own email, I use a signature file that contains the name of my site, its theme line, and my URL. This is automatically attached to the body of every message that I send.*

"404 Not Found" and Other Error Messages

Almost all web sites produce error messages. Whether they are an application bug generated by your middleware, the result of a bad search, or a "Page Not Found" error, these messages are all customizable. Make sure you take the time to craft human messages that will guide users back to where they belong. The "Page Not Found" error is a free marketing opportunity that some web developers miss out on or mis-use. Few savvy sites now leave the "404 Not Found" error alone; see Figure 4.14 for the default 404 messages that you'll see on some servers.

Most web developers take the time to customize this message in some way. But a surprising few really take advantage of this free marketing opportunity (see Figures 4.15 and 4.16). When you write these messages, try not to be cute or to overwhelm the user with too many options. Avoid the temptation to pontificate—just give the user what he needs: an obvious link to the home page, a way to contact you, links to frequently requested pages, and a *short and easy-to-understand* blurb on how the user might have gotten to the 404 page in the first place. The goal of all error messages should include keeping users on your site.

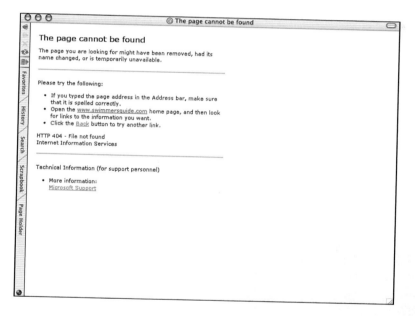

4.14   *Customize all error messages. Rarely do sites these days have a virgin "File Not Found" page. The customized 404 message is a free marketing tool available to even the barest budgets, and you will pay a penalty if you don't take advantage. When users come across broken URLs, whether you are responsible for them or not, you run the risk of losing their attention. If you have not customized your "Page Not Found" and other error messages, spend a little time doing it now.*

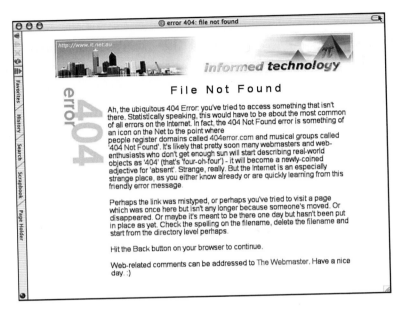

4.15 *Make sure all error messages are meaningful. This "Page Not Found" error is entertaining, but who is the page talking to? Not the customer. The entire first paragraph reads like the site developer is showing off or, worse, talking to herself. In the second paragraph, we begin to see some content that might be important to the reader. The best chance that users have for finding what they are looking for is in the last two paragraphs, but that information is not quite rich enough. Are the Back button and the email link all the help we can provide to the user? I think not. The goal of any copy, especially of the "Page Not Found" variety, should be to give users what they need. If you can do that and entertain the reader, that is even better: a dose of entertainment helps take the sting out of outdated links and other site-management errors. Just make sure you have the horse before the cart.*

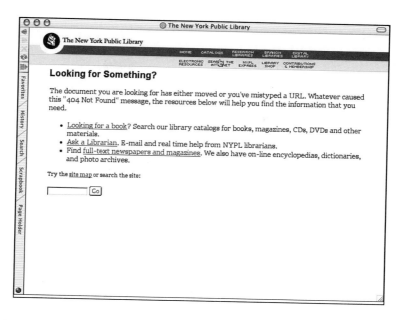

4.16 *This is a "Page Not Found" message that my colleague Catherine Jones and I wrote when we worked together for The Branch Libraries of The New York Public Library. Most of the language is based on frustrating experiences that we knew our users were having and on the site resources that we felt were of the best value to our users.*

Resources

If you are looking for 404 inspiration, visit these sites, dedicated to finding the best and the worst of the celebrated form:

- ☐ 404 Lounge: www.404lounge.net/
- ☐ 404 Research Lab: www.plinko.net/404/

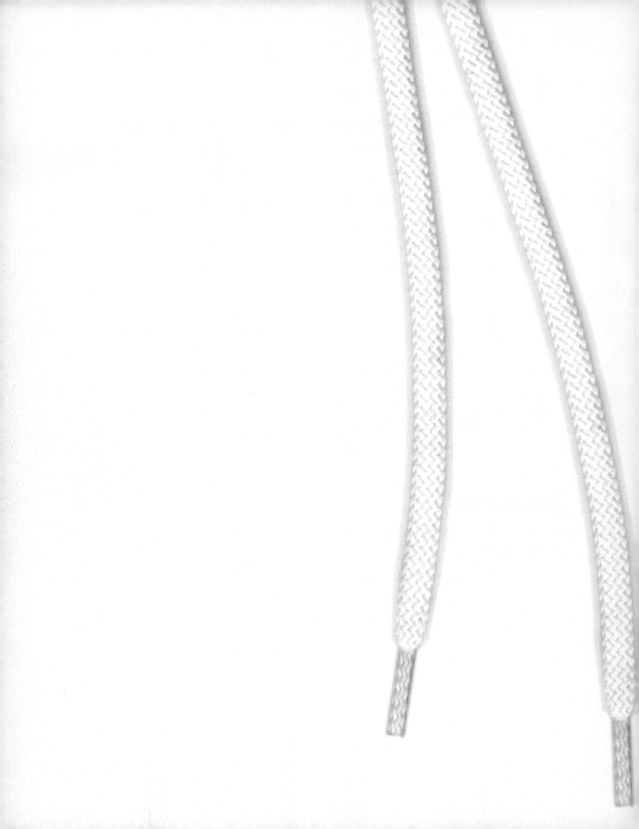

Chapter 5

The Design: Looking Good with Less

Chapter Checklist

1. **Economy is the key to good typography.**

   Limit the number of typefaces that you use.

2. **Stick to two or three well-chosen typefaces.**

   Make sure that they work well on the web and that together they provide nice contrast. Avoid typeface combinations that conflict or that look like ransom letters.

3. **Don't waste money on bad typefaces.**

   If you need a special typeface, use it in the branding area or masthead, and keep the rest of the typography straightforward.

4. **Save time and money with well-formed markup and external Cascading Style Sheets.**

   If you manage typography and color with CSS, your site will use less bandwidth and will be easier and less expensive to maintain than if you use messy font tags. (Details come in Chapter 7, "Save Time and Money with Web Standards.")

5. **For an elegant-looking site, stick to two or three good colors.**

   Even if your budget is $5,000, your site will look like a million bucks if you keep the palette clean and simple.

6. **You don't have to spend a bundle on photography and illustrations to give your site a polished look and feel.**

   When you select art, pick one style or treatment and stick with it. Crop and place art consistently. Begin with the highest-quality possible you can get .

> *❝ You know what you look like to me, with your good bag and your cheap shoes? You look like a rube. A well-scrubbed, hustling rube with a little taste.❞*
>
> —Hannibal Lecter to Clarice Starling in *The Silence of the Lambs* (1991)

I have a confession to make: I shop at discount stores for my professional wardrobe. I would like to think, however, that I do not look like I do. Perhaps I am kidding myself—or, more likely, I know the three keys to pulling it off.

The key to shopping at a discount store is threefold:

1. Define your style and stick to it.

2. Keep the color palette simple.

3. Keep the lines clean.

The same principles hold true for good-looking web sites. These principles will ensure that, even if you are working on a shoestring, you can deliver a polished, professional web site that looks like a million bucks.

It is easy to stroll into a discount clothing store such as Daffy's or TJ Maxx and walk out with stuff that nearly suits you but that does not help you put your best fashion foot forward. As you wade through all that merchandise, you might feel overwhelmed by the options, and pick up something that is ill fitting or a bad color for you. That might be fine for a pair of summer shorts. Who cares if you look a little funny if you wear them only while mowing the lawn? But a web site is among the most public endeavors that you and your client will ever undertake, and you want to make sure that no one is stuck out on the lawn with a serious case of plumber's butt.

With web design, there is no excuse for looking bad, even if you do not have much money. When you begin work on a small-budget site, do as fashion-conscious discount clothing buyers do: Define the style, stick to a simple color palette, and keep the lines clean. Let's look at how even on the smallest budget, consistent style, simple colors, and clean lines can be put to work with three core design elements: typography, color, and art.

Typography as a Three-Step Face-Lift

Imagine this scenario: You have just started a new job as an in-house web designer, and the first thing your boss wants you to do is clean up the web site. She has given you a week (and no money) to do it. This is not to be a complete redesign; that will come later when you have some cash. For now, you just need to give the site a face-lift.

Spinning Straw into Gold

Careful use of typography will elevate a cheap-looking site from garishness to sophistication, and you do not need to spend a dime! By limiting the number of typefaces on a site to two or three nicely contrasting faces, and by using the placement of text to create strong lines, your site will look more elegant and more expensive.

Assume that your cluttered site was created three years ago. Although it is fine as the boss's nephew's first web site, it makes your company look amateurish and out of touch.

Start with the typography and use it to define your style: Simplify your color scheme and clean up the visual lines in your site. Think about the variety of typefaces, how consistently each typeface is being used, and the placement of text on the screen. Ask yourself how you might change these three typographical elements—variety, consistent use, and placement—to eliminate visual clutter and to improve the site. This analysis begins a three-step face-lift that will inexpensively add elegance and style to any design you are trying to improve. Your boss will wish her Botox treatment had been as successful and pain-free.

1. **The careful variety of typefaces.** The least expensive way to create uniformity and hierarchy is to select two or three good typefaces. Try to select typefaces that together create strong visual contrast and that look good on a computer screen.

2. **The consistent use of typefaces.** After you have selected your typefaces, write a quick visual style guide that dictates how each of the typefaces will be used. This guide should prescribe a set of rules that cover elements such as headlines, site-wide navigation, body copy, links, and callouts. You will undoubtedly go back and make changes to these rules as you begin implementation. That is fine; just be sure to update your style guide.

3. **Creating clean lines by placing text.** When you lay out text on the screen, make sure that you use clean lines. What does this mean? It means that the elements on your page guide the viewer's eye from one place to the next via careful, balanced positioning, as explained later in this chapter. The alignment of each text area should be strong and should relate visually to other text areas on the page. Clean placement costs no more than sloppy placement, but it adds tremendously to the integrity of your design.

Assume that your short-term project is a site such as the one in Figure 5.1. Take the three elements—conservative variety of typefaces, consistent use of those typefaces, and clean lines via placement—and start cutting.

5.1 *Wholesale Wedding Bands (*www.WholesaleWeddingBands.com/*) has too many typefaces.*

The site pictured in Figure 5.1 would benefit immediately from our three-part face-lift. There are so many typefaces that it is hard to tell which part of the site is navigation, headline copy, body copy, or a special feature. No strong visual lines are used in the design, nor are there any other organizational clues. This leaves the user to wander haplessly about the page, having to create her own sense of how the various materials are organized.

For a sneak preview of the site's potential, see Figure 5.2, which shows this site after our three-part face-lift.

Note

This site reminds me of a 14-color eye shadow kit that my Aunt Maureen gave me when I was a teenager. Overwhelmed by all the cosmetic options, I managed to use seven shades on my right eyelid and the other seven on my left. Maureen noticed my error, took me aside, and showed me how to make use of two complementary colors that would add definition to my eyes. The principles she gave me apply to our site: Scale back and use only those visual elements that do a particular job.

A note to people who live in glass houses: The site's owner is also the site's designer. This mother of eight and grandmother of six bought an HTML book and put the site together herself. The first site I built was no better than this one. I use Wholesale Wedding Bands as an example of the first- and second-generation sites that people like us are hired to redesign.

The Number of Typefaces

The Wholesale Wedding Bands home page sports at least 10 different typefaces. Together they create visual conflict that undermines the site's message and functionality. It is difficult to distinguish highlights, headings, and site navigation from plain old copy.

The trouble with this particular site is that it uses text as decoration. The wedding theme has inspired the Wholesale Wedding Band designer to run wild with script and decorative typefaces. It's fine to select a typeface that subtly suggests a mood, but it is unwise to use it as decoration. Unless you have the time and skill to pull off such concepts, this decorative approach can be the fast track to looking cheap. While you are scaling back, kill the cute stuff.

As you identify two or three typefaces that you will use for the site, consider the following convention that print and web designers have always used: Select a serif typeface such as Times or Georgia for the copy, and a sans serif typeface such as Verdana, Helvetica, or Arial for the headers and navigational elements. (But be aware of problems discussed in the sidebar.) If you prefer, you can do the opposite: Use sans serif for the copy and serif for the header elements. You might sparingly use a decorative typeface for the logo.

Definition: Serif Typeface

A serif typeface is defined by the presence of a descender—the short, angular line that stems from the upper and lower ends of the strokes of a letter. Serif typefaces, also called Roman typefaces, are good for many purposes in the print world, especially for large bodies of text. They can be tricky on a computer monitor, though; the detail of the serif stroke can look jagged on some screens due to their low resolution compared to the printed page. As computer monitors improve, serif typefaces will become a better option for just about any element on a web site; for now, though, I like to reserve them for page elements such as headers and headlines. There is an exception to every rule: Microsoft's Georgia serif face was specifically designed to work well on low-resolution computer screens, and it comes preinstalled on most Windows and Macintosh operating systems.

Examples of serif typefaces are Times New Roman, Georgia, and Palatino.

Definition: Sans Serif Typeface

Sans is French for "without." A sans serif typeface is one without the descender lines emanating from the strokes of a letter. Again, what is true in the print world is not necessarily so on a computer screen. In print, sans serif typefaces are often reserved for headlines and callouts. On the web, their clean, unfussy lines are eminently readable and, therefore, make them perfect for body copy. Note that of the examples listed next, Verdana is the most legible and most reader-friendly, particularly at smaller sizes. Like Georgia, Verdana was designed for the screen by Matthew Carter and is available on most Windows and Macintosh computers. Impact, which also comes with most Mac and Windows computers, can be a powerful headline face but is of no use for body copy. (In your CSS, set Impact's font-weight to normal to avoid artificially "double-bolding" this already bold typeface.)

Examples of sans serif typefaces are Arial, Verdana, and **Impact**.

Definition: Decorative and Script Typeface

I am lumping decorative and script typefaces together for this discussion. Know, however, that decorative typefaces are oddballs that do not fit squarely into other type categories. Their job is to do just what their name suggests: to decorate. Script typefaces resemble handwriting and, like decorative typefaces, are best used in small doses. Limit the use of decorative and script typefaces to logos and isolated bits of branding; they are just too hard to read for copy and navigation areas.

Examples of decorative and script typefaces are *Bickham Script*, **Bermuda LP**, and **Hobo Std**.

For more about the classification of typefaces, see Adobe's *Typography Basics: Typeface Classification* (`www.adobe.com/support/techguides/printpublishing/ typography_basics/typeface_classifications/main.html`). The point of view is that of a print designer, so keep in mind that some suggestions about implementation will not work for the web.

The Consistent Use of Typefaces

When you have selected a core set of typefaces, it is time to think carefully about how to use the faces consistently. To do this successfully, analyze the content areas on your page:

- What is the most important element in the site pictured in Figure 5.1? Is it the company name? The theme line? Is there more than one theme line? Is "Wholesale Wedding Bands, where you pay for the ring, not the salesman's commission" the theme line? The message is a strong one, and it is stated clearly, but the choice of typeface waters it down.
- What are the site's navigational elements? How can they be organized and type-set in a way that makes it clear to the visitor that these items are navigational rather than body copy or callouts?

As you write the style guide that defines the rules for type treatment, you will be making the answers to these questions clear.

Your style guide might look like the one shown in Table 5.1. Note that I have selected three typefaces: a serif typeface for headers, headlines, and specials; a sans serif typeface for navigation and body copy; and a decorative typeface for the logo and branding. Each typeface will be used differently. That variation will add some of the contrast that users need to distinguish page elements. Body copy, links, and left and top navigation will all use the same typeface, but color, weight, and size will vary.

Note also that I have a column on the right called "CSS Rule." We'll make use of that column in Chapter 7.

Table 5.1	A Sample Style Guide				
	Typeface*	Size	Color**	Weight	CSS Rule
Headlines/ Header	Georgia, Times New Roman, Times, serif	Header 1: 18px Header 2: 16px Header 3: 15px Header 4: 13px	#330066 (purple)	Bold	
Top Navigation	Verdana, Arial, Helvetica, sans serif	14px	#000066 (blue)	Bold	
Left Navigation	Verdana, Arial, Helvetica, sans serif	12px	#000066 (blue)	Bold	
Logo/Branding	Zapfino	18px, sharp antialiased	#6633CC (lavender)	Normal	
Specials	Georgia, Times New Roman, Times, serif	14px	#330066 (purple)	Bold	
Body Copy	Verdana, Arial, Helvetica, sans serif	12px	#000033 (dark blue)	Normal	
Links in Body Copy	Verdana, Arial, Helvetica, sans serif	12px	#6633CC (lavender)	Bold, underlined	

* Under "Typeface," I have a list of faces. This is because typefaces vary among operating systems and browsers. I address this later under "Implementation of Typography."

** Colors are listed not only by the name of the color, but also by the hexadecimal value for that color. This is because most color on the web is expressed in hex. This style guide makes it easy to keep track of these six character values.

Remember that one typeface offers many options. Weight, size, and color are waiting for you to play with them. Use them—they will add necessary contrast to your design. Such contrast is not only visually pleasing, but it is also informative: It helps the busy visitor scan the page and determine which elements are most important.

Placing Text

The use of typography in Figure 5.2 (my quick redesign of the Wholesale Wedding Bands site) is effective and economical. By reducing the number of typefaces to three and the columns to two, three strong lines are created. One line is to the leftmost edge of the site, one is the line created by the left edge of the photo and customer comments, and the last line is the right edge of the page. Justifying the text in the customer comments and in the top navigation helps the right line remain strong. Notice how the alignment of text in this site does a much better job of creating strong vertical lines. This makes the site much easier to read and use. This redesigned site might or might not have been built on a budget, but it does not feel cheap.

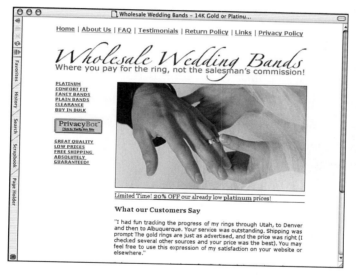

5.2 *Wholesale Wedding Bands redesigned. Simply by limiting the number of typefaces and by using text to create strong lines, I have successfully implemented the three keys to looking good. I created a simple style and used it consistently, I simplified the color scheme, and I placed text in a way that creates strong lines.*

I also reduced visual clutter by simplifying the site. Creating more screen real estate supplies enough room to move the customer comments up a bit; before the redesign, this valuable copy was below the fold.

Implementation of Typography

As you work on the typographical aspect of any design, keep in mind two important implementation issues:

1. A limited number of typefaces are common across all browsers and operating systems.

2. The only way to guarantee that users will see the typeface that you want them to see is to use images of text rather than XHTML text. This practice is sometimes advisable and sometimes not, as discussed a few paragraphs from now.

These two points are at odds with one another, and you will need to find a balance. If budget is your worry, reconciling this tension is pretty straightforward.

Typefaces Across Browsers and Operating Systems

As you set about implementing your design, keep in mind that few typefaces are common across all browsers and operating systems. For text to render with the typeface that you selected, that font must be on your users' machines.

Look back for a moment to Table 5.1, which shows a list of typefaces for each text element. Headers will display in Georgia if the user has that font on his computer. (Nearly all Windows and Mac users have it.) If not, headers will display in Times New Roman. If the user has none of the fonts listed on his computer, the headers will display in whatever serif font happens to be on that computer. Under extraordinarily rare circumstances, if the user has no serif fonts, a default system font will be used. Remember to select a range of typefaces for each text element.

Depending on the fonts available on a given platform, you will want to specify the preferred font face first, then acceptable alternative faces, and then the default. For example, the Classic Mac OS includes Helvetica, but, for small text, many Mac users prefer Geneva, which is not traditionally available on Windows; you want to specify Geneva first to ensure that Mac users don't get the less desirable Helvetica.

Controlling Typefaces with Images

In the Wholesale Wedding Bands example, I selected Zapfino as the decorative typeface for the site's logo. You can bet your bottom dollar that the Zapfino font is not going to be on every receiving device that visits the site. I do, however, want to make sure that all visitors see the logo in Zapfino. The only way I can guarantee this is if I create the logo with an image editor such as Adobe Photoshop or Macromedia Fireworks (see Figure 5.3) and export it as a text GIF in Photoshop's Save for Web dialog box. Then I must include that image in my XHTML page.

Budget Threat

Adobe Photoshop is not cheap, nor is the alternative, Macromedia Fireworks. But nothing else compares to these products when it comes to producing professional-looking graphics. In the case of image editors, I am not going to suggest an inexpensive alternative; spend the money. If you skimp on image editors, your site will suffer.

If you do use images for text, be sure to provide alternative (alt) text for devices that lack support for graphics so that the title of the page or name of the company isn't completely absent on those devices. Backing every image with alt attribute text will help you and your users, and it may also, in a few cases, make your site's content more accessible to some search engines.

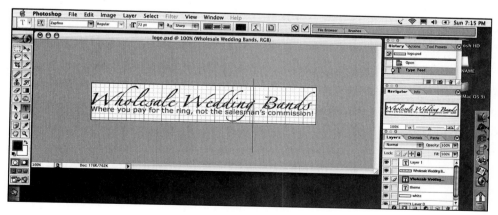

5.3 *Here's the logo file image as I am working on it in PhotoShop. I can create an image using any fonts that I have on my system and then export that file as a GIF image to be used in my web site. This is a common practice among web designers.*

Budget Threat

Image files might make your site require more bandwidth to download, which translates into wasted time for the people visiting your site with a slow connection. In extreme cases, when too many images are used, some visitors will tire of waiting and leave, defeating the purpose of creating a web site in the first place and, for a business or commerce site, potentially resulting in lost revenue. Also, if your web-hosting company charges you for data transfer, you could see an increase in your hosting expenses if you use too many bandwidth-gobbling images.

Another cost to worry about is the expense of production and maintenance of these images. Each image takes time to create, optimize, update, and then optimize again. Any time I wanted to make a change to the text in Figure 5.3, I would have to open that image in an editor, save the changes, optimize the image, and then put the replacement GIF image back on my server. If I could have used text, I might save a step or two. This hardly matters when your site contains just a few images, but as you add more images that contain vital content that must frequently be updated, you might see production costs go up needlessly.

One might argue that I have overstated the problems that come with using images for text. True enough. There are ways to work with images that avoid these difficulties with transfer rates and production costs: First, reduce the file size of each image as much as possible. Photoshop's Save for Web dialog makes it easy to do that without losing quality. Then keep in mind that repeated images are cached on the user's hard drive, saving the user transfer time (and saving you hosting costs) when visiting more than one page on your site. It is not a mortal or even venial sin to use images this way; just make sure that you are not using text images gratuitously. When you use them, use them well.

Text GIF images are appropriate for logos and, in some cases, might even be appropriate for subheads. But most web text, including subheads, is better handled as XHTML markup styled with Cascading Style Sheets, discussed next.

Save Time and Money with Cascading Style Sheets

Plan on using Cascading Style Sheets to control typography. This will not only cut storage and transfer costs when you serve the site, but it also will make the site easier to maintain and will cut the labor costs when you eventually and inevitably redesign.

Cascading Style Sheets (CSS) provide a standard way of controlling the layout and design of web documents. We go into CSS in greater detail in Chapter 7, but the general idea is this: Remove all presentation work from your XHTML, and let a style sheet do that work for you. Also remove font tags, spacer GIF images, and other presentational tags and attributes, and let your style sheet do this work for you.

Definition: Presentation

When I talk about "presentation" in a web site, I mean the way your pages look in the browser. In subtle and sometimes not-so-subtle ways, presentation can vary from one device or platform or browser to another, whether you like it or not. You have some, but not perfect, control over this.

Definition: Structure

When I talk about the "structure" of an XHTML page, ideally I mean the logical structure that you give it in markup. The idea is to remove all presentational tags and attributes from the XHTML and reduce your markup to the simplest, most logical elements. CSS then adds a presentational layer to that markup when your page hits the browser. If this is too much too soon, just let these ideas float around in your head until you hit Chapter 7.

This is a different way of formatting than the method we web designers grew up with. In the old days, we had to style each paragraph with its own font tag and style each headline with its own font tag. It was like walking to school uphill both ways. With CSS, you keep your XHTML clean and simple, and you define a paragraph or header's style in your CSS document. This takes much less work, and your production, maintenance, and redesign consequently go much faster—which should be music to the ears of overworked, underfinanced shoestring designers everywhere.

If you build your site efficiently—use external rather than embedded or inline style sheets, and leverage the power of good markup—your pages will be smaller. This will save on data transfer (a.k.a. bandwidth) costs. You will see the real savings when you begin your HTML markup; this process is exponentially faster when you use CSS to do the presentation work.

Implementation of CSS

Here you'll learn how you can use CSS to meet your one-week deadline, and we set the stage for bandwidth savings. The first thing to do is remove all font tags. Figure 5.4 shows the HTML markup behind Figure 5.1, the Wholesale Wedding Bands site before its redesign. As seen in Lines 54 and 63, the font tags are all over this site, eating up bandwidth, and they do not need to be there. If they are in your site, take them out and let CSS do that work for you.

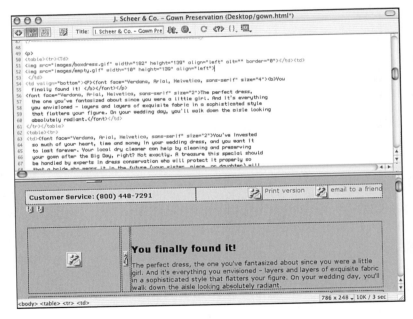

5.4 *The source of Figure 5.1 reveals a site that is controlled with outdated, time- and bandwidth-wasting font tags and spacer GIF images. A more economical approach is to let Cascading Style Sheets do this design work.*

This site has a few more gratuitous HTML tags that waste resources. The XHTML of the redesign reduces it from 28KB of markup to 4KB, plus a 2KB style sheet. In Chapter 7, you'll return to this example and use this same site as an exercise in leaner, less expensive markup.

In Line 52 of Figure 5.4, you see the ubiquitous spacer GIF. Since the days of Netscape 1.1, designers have been using spacer images to add margins and padding to their sites. The spacer tag was introduced in NS Navigator 3.0, but as early as 1995, designers were using transparent GIF images to hold designs together. The big problem with using those images in those days was that, depending on its configuration, Netscape tried to fetch them every time they were referenced by a page. A site that used transparent GIFs liberally consumed too much bandwidth.

This practice still wastes bandwidth by populating the web with a bazillion of these vacant little images and by writing markup that refers to them. Here is a money-saving tip: *Cut it out.*

If you need a margin between page elements, you can create it in your style sheet. If you need to have a right margin on just one image and you don't want it to appear on other images in your site, write an inline style just for that. We cover this and more in Chapter 7.

Saving with CSS: A Real-World Example

When I came to my new job in The Digital Library program at The New York Public Library, we needed to give one of our small sites a face-lift (see Figure 5.5). We had a budget of nothing and no time to do the work. There was no time to create a new brand, nor was there time to create even new images. The solution that we chose was to stick with our existing art and logo, and to clean up the text of the site with a style sheet.

This is what the two-day production schedule looked like:

Day 1:

- Modify an existing style sheet. (2 hours)
- Clean up old, deprecated HTML markup and replace it with elegant, structural XHTML. (4 hours)

Day 2:

- ☐ Test on various browsers and operating systems. See how the site looks on target browsers and operating systems (see more on target browsers in Chapter 2, "The Pound Wise Project Plan"). As you will learn in Chapter 7, this kind of testing is faster and more efficient when you use CSS. (4 hours)
- ☐ Launch.

The result was a cleaner, more cohesive-looking site (see Figure 5.6). We used the color from the existing art for the link and header elements. We also added leading and indentation to the paragraph element to make the copy more readable. The work took about 10 hours and was split between two people who performed their tasks when they were not toiling on their main project. The style sheet was based on one from an earlier project, so development was fast.

5.5 *This is the Digital Library Program site before the two-day cleanup.*

5.6 *Here is the same Digital Library Program site after the easy, CSS-based two-day cleanup.*

As described, this work was a temporary fix; we will be working with a designer in the next few months to develop a new logo and an entirely new look. If we had not been using CSS to do this temporary job, I would have considered this task bad use of time. But now that we have clean XHTML and a friendlier, more legible, more usable design that is handled by CSS, we are better prepared to make the transition to the final, improved design to come. Using CSS and cleaning up our markup not only saved us time and money on a temporary, transitional redesign; it will also save time and money on the true redesign because the site is now in better shape, with its biggest problems solved in-house on a shoestring budget and timeline.

Less-Is-More Color

When you work on a shoestring budget, the trick to color is to keep it simple and to remember that there are no bad colors, just bad color combinations.

If you have to manage a whole site on a small budget, you probably do not have an entire design team to do subtle work with color, nor do you have time to test your palette on a variety of computers. If you are short on resources in this way, avoid using too many colors. Going over two or three shades increases your chances of producing a garish site.

The secret to an elegant look is to stick to two or three good colors. This technique, along with typographical restraint, will keep your site looking timeless and elegant. Think Grace Kelley instead of Cyndi Lauper.

To reinforce the value of a simple palette, visit two of my favorite sites, shown in Figures 5.7 and 5.8.

5.7   *The Clinique site keeps colors simple (www.clinique.com). The trademark green does most of the heavy lifting, while subtle use of brown, beige, and pinks provides visual contrast.*

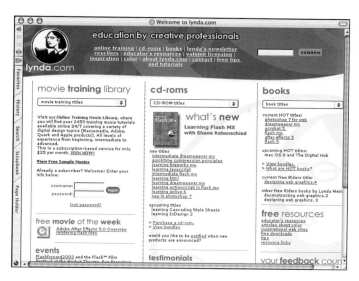

5.8 *Designer and educator Lynda Weinman has always had a beautiful site
(*`www.lynda.com/resources/inspiration/`*). It has changed several times, but each
time Lynda has used color with great economy. She tends to use two related colors
at a time. She also maintains a list of sites that use colors in this same way.*

Each of these sites uses a simple palette of two or three main colors. Clinique's
main color is the green that you see on all of its personal care products. Supporting
and tertiary colors draw upon the colors in their product line. Lipstick pages, for
example, suggest the season's new shades. Powder and foundation pages pick up on
the beige and browns of those products. This much color could be a stretch for a
shoestring budget; the production and maintenance costs associated with page-by-
page art direction might be beyond your means. My guess is that people reading
this book do not have time to handcraft production at such a detailed level. The
inexpensive way to achieve the same balanced effect is to work with something more
like Lynda Weinman's color scheme. Lynda's headers are in pale lavender, and her links
and art are in a related blue. I'm not suggesting that you copy Lynda's colors, but
rather that you learn from her skilled use of just a few related colors.

Easier Color with CSS

Again, CSS is the best way to manage the color of your site. You'll see in Chapter 7 how to control text, links, backgrounds, and even rollover colors with Cascading Style Sheets. When redesign time rolls around, much of your work can be done in the few minutes it takes to change a style sheet.

Art and Photography

Art and photography can be expensive. Often when designers try to cut corners here, their sites look cheap. Figure 5.9 shows an inspired but poorly executed attempt to save money. The background of the site is a photograph of lacy fabric like you would see in a wedding dress. It looks as though the designer captured a bolt of lace on a flatbed scanner. The lace is a bit overexposed and out of focus. The use of the lace image is rather self-aware, calling unnecessary attention to a far too literal design element. The result? Darn it, the site just feels a bit tacky. The small-budget vibe that it sends out would make me reluctant to entrust a thousand-dollar garment in this company's care; they seem to like to cut corners. Will they do that with my dress?

The execution of this particular lace image adds an unnecessary expense: The image is a whopping 140KB. This is a huge file to ask your users to download, and it is a big file to host if you have to pay for data transfer rates, (a.k.a. bandwidth consumption). You might not be able to afford sending 140KB (see Chapter 8, "Bang-for-Your-Buck Hosting and Domains," for more on transfer rates and bandwidth costs). And even if you can afford it, your dial-up users probably can't. 140KB is more than 40 times the file size you should aim for in a background image.

5.9 *Poorly produced art used too literally undermines the service you are trying to sell (www.after-the-event.co.uk). The lacy background image in this wedding dress preservation page looks amateurish; would a customer send an heirloom garment to an amateur? Inexpensive art does not have to look cheap, but when it does, your site and your brand suffer, and so might your bottom line.*

This is not to say that background images are always a bad idea. My warning is really about how you produce any image files that you use on your site.

- **Make sure that the image quality is as high as possible.** If you can't get the focus and exposure crisp enough, find a stock-art source that can do it for you.

- **Make sure that the file size is small.** Try to aim for less than 3K, or even smaller for an image that is just an enhancement and that is not critical to the site's message.

- **If you use a background, follow the steps on using external style sheets to display background images in Chapter 7.** This is more economical for your hosting demands and is easier on your users who are stuck with slow Internet connections.

Be Careful with Clip Art

Clip art is tricky business; it is easy to get carried away by the decorative potential of this genre. Try not to let it happen. Instead, remember that clip art is best used in small doses as iconography that helps users quickly scan your site. Remember our keys to looking good for less: Pick one style and stick it with it, keep colors simple, and create lines that are strong and consistent. To that end, the goal with any clip art should be twofold:

1. **Create visual harmony.** Find art that is consistent in style, weight, perspective, and color. Try to select art that looks like it is also from the same time period.
2. **Work with high-quality images.** Find art with as high a resolution as possible, and then scale it back to the size and resolution that you need. Art is easier to work with if you begin with a high-quality, high-resolution file.

Let's look at some examples (shown in Figures 5.10, 5.11, and 5.12) that do this unsuccessfully and successfully.

**Clip art goal 1,
visual harmony: yes**

**Clip art goal 2,
image quality: no**

5.10 *Hendersonville County Public Library (www.henderson.lib.nc.us) achieves the first clip-art goal well; each icon agrees in terms of style, weight, perspective, and color. The quality of the art, however, leaves something to be desired. It looks as though the designer started with low-resolution images and edited those low-quality files. The result is the jagged look; the images need to be sharper. Have you ever listened to a tape of a tape of a tape of your favorite music? You notice an appreciable loss of sound quality. The same happens when you use a low-quality image; if you can work from a high-resolution "master," the file that you finish with will be of a much better quality. Before I leave this site, I have to point out something remarkable: The library director's phone number is posted clearly in the top of the page. Now that's customer service.*

**Clip art goal 1,
visual harmony: no**

**Clip art goal 2,
image quality: yes**

5.11 *Rather than pick from a series of disparate clip art styles, the designer of the Mansfield/Richmond Count Public Library site (www.mrcpl.lib.oh.us) might have selected just one of these styles and used it consistently. The calendar and computer icons are intended to help the user quickly scan and prioritize information, but because each piece of art is different in terms of size, weight, shadow, perspective, and color, they add clutter to an already visually noisy page. Mansfield/Richmond does a good job with the second clip-art goal: The image quality is high. But the site falls short in the first clip-art goal: It desperately needs visual harmony.*

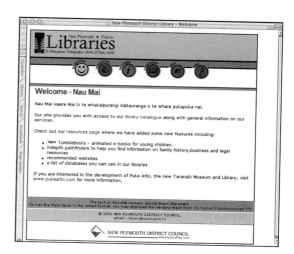

**Clip art goal 1,
visual harmony: yes**

**Clip art goal 2,
image quality: yes**

5.12 *The New Plymouth District Libraries site (www.pukeariki.com/npdl/) uses clip art that comes from a high-quality source and that creates visual harmony. On closer examination, each icon in the top navigation appears to be from a different source: some look like they are from a font set and others look like they are from a clip art set. They work together, however, because the designer has given them similar weight and size, and has accorded them the same circle treatment. Even the placement of text on the top left of each icon adds balance and consistency to this design. Clip art works most effectively when it is used harmoniously; the art gets out of the way of the navigational job it has to do.*

Finding Cheap Clip Art

The problems we see in the Hendersonville County and Mansfield/Richmond County Public Library sites tend to arise when designers scour the web for clip art. Do a quick Google search on Free Library Clip Art, and you'll see what I mean. So much clip art is available that it makes it hard to find the good stuff. Finding a set of images that come with high-resolution files and create visual harmony is hard if you limit yourself to the web. You have to separate the wheat from the chaff, which is a time-consuming and expensive process. A few sources can make the process a bit easier.

Clip Art on the Web

I turn to several sources when I need to find clip art on the web, including Veer (see Figure 5.13). Some are free; others ask for money (see Table 5.2). As you would expect, the more you pay, the higher the quality, but there are ways to stretch the value of a buck when you use the more expensive sources.

Table 5.2	Clip Art Guide		
Company	Cost	Good News	Bad News
ClipArt.com (www.clipart.com)	Subscriptions range from about $8 per week to $150 per year. You can download whatever (and as much as) you want, with no additional per-item charge.	The price is low, the selection is large, and you can download high-resolution images. The site also offers fonts, photography, and other resources.	There is more bad art than good, so you will spend quite a bit of time winnowing, and time is money. Also, you will have to work hard to select images that agree in terms of style, weight, perspective, and color.
Veer (www.veer.com)	A single image can cost $100 or more, and a collection of images can cost $200 or more.	It is easy to find a clip art set that meets both of our goals (visual harmony and high image quality). Veer also offers photography, fonts, and a whole mess of visual resources.	

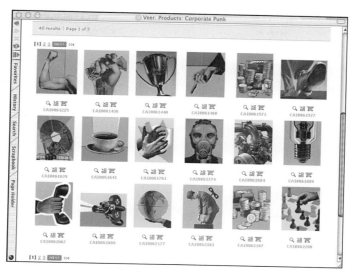

5.13 *Veer (www.veer.com) is an example of the kind of material you can find at the better art sites. We have crossed the line from clip art to a higher class: stock art (some of the images here might be used for clip art, though). This particular collection is called Corporate Punk. You can buy the set of 40 business scenarios from Veer's web site for about $350. This might seem like a lot of money, but you get a high-quality set of images that create visual harmony when used together. Consider the time it would take to make painstakingly selected free clip art work as well. Can you afford the labor? You can use these images repeatedly in many different applications.*

Clip Art Libraries

You also can buy art libraries on CD. Art Explosion (www.hallogram.com/artexplosion/) is a set I have used many times. This set of CDs is available for Windows or Mac, and it usually goes for about $100 or $200, depending on the size of the collection. I just saw a set of 10,000 images sell on eBay (www.ebay.com) for about $10. Buy the largest set you can afford; you will use the material many times.

Dingbat Fonts

As you try to save money on clip art, don't forget about the dingbat, or symbol fonts sets, that are probably already on your computer. These are font sets that contain symbols rather than letters. Webdings and Wingdings are two that ship with most personal computers. You can purchase dingbat font sets such as Big Cheese or ZeitGuys for about $60 from a foundry such as Emigre (`www.emigre.com`). You can also find less interesting but free dingbat fonts by doing a web search on the phrases *freeware dingbat* or *symbol fonts*.

The advantage to using dingbat font sets over clip art libraries and web sites is that it is easier to achieve visual harmony: A single dingbat font set contains a large set of symbols that look nice together. The other great thing about dingbat fonts is that, because they are vector based, they are as high-quality and high-resolution as you need them to be. You can type them into any image editor (Photoshop, Fireworks) and scale them to any size, and they stay crisp as a winter morning. For this to work, make sure that the fonts you buy are scaleable. In other words, purchase PostScript, TrueType, or Open Type fonts.

High-quality bitmap fonts, such as those available at Joe Gillespie's MiniFonts site (`www.minifonts.com`), are perfect for some web design jobs, but by their nature, bitmap fonts do not scale: They are intended to be used at one size only or at an exact multiple of that size. (For instance, a 10px bitmap dingbat can also be used at 20px or 30px, but not at 14px.)

Finding Affordable Photography and Fine Art

Clip art can be nice, and it can even be a shoestring designer's best friend, but it has its limits. If you desire a polished brand image, you will need more than cute icons. But professional photography and fine art are expensive. A nice 10-page site can easily eat up a $1,000 art budget. How can you get around that cost?

What do you have in your file cabinets and desk drawers? Check your organization's old annual reports and brochures for art. Talk to your colleagues about photo shoots that might have been undertaken for some other purpose. You might find that some of this work has been done for you. As you look for existing material, keep two things in mind:

1. Just because your company used a piece of art for print does not mean you have the right to use it on the web. Find out who really owns the item, and make sure you have permission. Remember that scavenging for repurposable artwork like this can be a copyright nightmare; if you do not do your home-work well, you could pay big bucks later in legal costs if the artist (rightfully) comes after you. If you are not sure that you have permission to use a piece of art, just skip it. When working with your organization's previously published materials, those who produced the old brochures or annual reports can tell you what their contractual agreements with the photographers allow.

2. Be careful about scanning from a paper brochure; you could wind up with an image that looks bad. Try to get your hands on the original photographic slide or digitized image file.

Definition: Royalty-Free

Royalty-free images are not free. *Royalty-free* means that you can buy and outright own the right to use an image. You then can use that image as many times as you want at no addi-tional charge. You do not have exclusive rights to the image; anyone else who pays the fee can use the same photograph or artwork.

Definition: Rights-Managed

Rights-managed images are images that you pay for every time you use them. The cost of use depends on how you use an image and how long you will need to use it. I have used rights-managed images on large web sites, and the labor cost of simply managing rights was expen-sive. We needed one full-time staff member just to keep records; that is expensive work. For shoestring designers, royalty-free photos and artwork are the most cost-effective choice, in more ways than one.

If the search for in-house photography fails you, try some inexpensive and free image libraries (see Table 5.3). Most of the clip art resources that I listed previously also sell fine art and photography (see Figures 5.14 and 5.15).

Table 5.3 Photo and Fine Art Guide			
Company	**Cost**	**Good News**	**Bad News**
The New York Public Library's Digital Gallery (http://digital.nypl.org/imagegate/)	Free.	This is a big database, and it is growing. The site should contain about 600,000 images by 2004. New images are added on a regular basis. Nearly everything in this collection is out of copyright.	Because nearly everything is out of copyright, you will not find current photography. If you need to order a high-resolution image, it might take a while, and there could be a handling fee.
The American Memory Project at the Library of Congress (http://memory.loc.gov/)	Free.	This broad collection of materials relates to the history of the United States. Images are just one kind of material you'll find here. Books, music, and photographs of 3D objects are also included. I use this site when I need an illustration of something such as a banjo to work from.	Like at NYPL's Digital Gallery, you will not find recent material.
Rebel Artist (www.rebelartist.com)	About $3 an image.	Rebel Artist offers a pretty good collection of clip art and typefaces, as well as photographs.	You will not find anything as fine as you would with a more expensive stock art library.
Istockphoto (www.iStockphoto.com)	A download credit costs 25¢.	You can buy packages of credits in $10, $20, $50, and $100 amounts. This is a collection of low-cost, good-quality, royalty-free files contributed by site members. High-resolution downloads cost 25¢ and allow you to use a photograph in commercial web and print publications. If you are a photographer, you can become a member. If you contribute your own images, you get credits toward image purchases.	Although it is continually growing, the selection is small compared to the selection at Getty Images or Veer.com, and there are not many words to search on. The same organization also offers istockpro (www.iStockpro.com), whose images are of higher and more consistent quality.
Getty Images (www.gettyimages.com)	$25 and up—way up.	You can find beautiful photographs and illustrations that will make your site look like a million bucks. Spending a little money here for a key part of your site could pay off well.	Just the cost. Limit your search to royalty-free images. Rights-managed images could cost too much.
Veer (www.veer.com)	Comparable to Getty Images.	Veer's service is similar to Getty Images and was started by people who had worked at a division of Getty. Quality and variety are superb.	Same as with Getty Images.

5.14 *Istockphoto (www.istockphoto.com) is my favorite source for royalty-free images. If you begin to create your own stock photography, you can sell it here. A popular photograph can bring the artist a couple hundred dollars.*

5.15 *Getty Images (www.gettyimages.com) sells both rights-managed and royalty-free images; if you are tight on cash, limit your search to royalty-free images.*

Spinning Straw into Gold

Shoestring designers, take heart! If cost is the limiting factor and you have access to a digital camera, you can get some decent art by taking it yourself and working image-editing magic in Photoshop or Fireworks.

For a branded and professional appearance, use your photographs creatively and consistently. If you had to shoot under a variety of lighting conditions and the color balance varies from photo to photo, Photoshop's Variations or Hue and Saturation dialog boxes (found in the Adjustment section of the Image menu) can help bring consistency to these disparate sources.

Or, you might use Photoshop's Desaturate filter (Image, Adjustments, Desaturate) to remove the color from your images, and then use Variations to tint all photos in one or more colors that complement your site's design palette.

In addition to consistency in lighting and color, be consistent with the way you crop your photos. If you crop in tight on three portraits and use a long shot for the fourth portrait, your design will lose energy and integrity. If you crop all subjects the same way, the content of your images will achieve a professionalism that belies the low budget behind the camera.

An inexpensive digital camera can produce photographs that are good enough and of high enough resolution for the web. In fact, you might want to begin taking photographs to build your own stock photography library. Bruce Livingstone, the man behind Istockphoto, recently published *A Designer's Guide to Making Your Own Stock Photography* (for nonphotographers) at *Digital Web Magazine* (www.digital-web.com/features/feature_2002-03.shtml). He shows you how to use a $20 medium-format camera to produce your own art.

Making the Most of Bad Art

A small budget can mean that you are just stuck with bad art. When that happens, make sure that you treat the art consistently.

I recently spoke with designer and author Sandee Cohen (see Figure 5.16). We discussed the fact that stock art and photography can be expensive. I asked her if she had ways to work around that cost. What do you do when you don't want your site to look like a bargain basement, but you can't afford to pay hundreds of dollars for photography?

Sandee's answer sums up the solution well:

"It's not the artwork, but what you do with it. There are loads of techniques to jazz up rather mundane clip art or stock photos in Photoshop or any image-editing program. I'm probably the cheapest person on the planet. I remember buying a CD for $20 many years ago with loads of images on it. All by themselves, they look cheap. But run a few filters on them, and they look cool."

5.16 *Sandee also writes a monthly column of tips, tricks, and techniques called "The Digital Dish" (*www.creativepro.com*). She speaks and teaches all over the United States, and she maintains her personal web site, Vector Babe (*www.vectorbabe.com*). This is a great site to visit from time to time; I find Sandee's solid and practical advice especially apt for those of us on a budget.*

I worked on a small-scale educational site where we put Sandee's principles to use. We used the typographical and color principles outlined previously; we had a nice-looking site with strong lines and two complementary colors: teal and ocher. (For the guys, that's blue-green and dark orange.)

One of the main sections of the site was a teacher biography area. The main visual element of these pages was a teacher-submitted photograph. You can imagine that the quality and style of the snapshots were wide ranging. Most were taken with low-resolution digital cameras, and a few teachers mailed us 3 × 5 snapshots from their last vacation. None of the shots looked that good. Had we simply slapped these shots into the site as is, we would have had a look like the one you saw earlier in Figure 5.9. But we took a few minutes on this two-step process, as you can see in Figures 5.17, 5.18, and 5.19.

5.17, 5.18, and 5.19 *Try this when you have to work with inconsistent and low-quality photography. These photographs have been cropped so that they occupy the same horizontal space. They have also been treated similarly: They each have a 1px wide green stroke as a border. This stroke helps integrate these photos with the site and lends a hint of harmony to otherwise disparate photographs (*`www.nyp.org`*).*

What did we do?

1. We cropped each photo so that it was the same width and so that the teachers appeared in more or less the same proportions.
2. We gave the photos a 1px teal border.

The results were not perfect. If we had been able to conduct the photo shoot instead of simply receiving people's snapshots, we could have placed the teachers in similar environments, with consistent lighting conditions, and shot them from approximately the same distance, using the same focal length. If we had been able to do that, the images could have been cropped at identical aspect ratios instead of merely at the same width. Still, given what we had to work with, we were able to create a strong site. Even if you are stuck with a budget of nothing for art, you can take a few minutes and make the best of what you have.

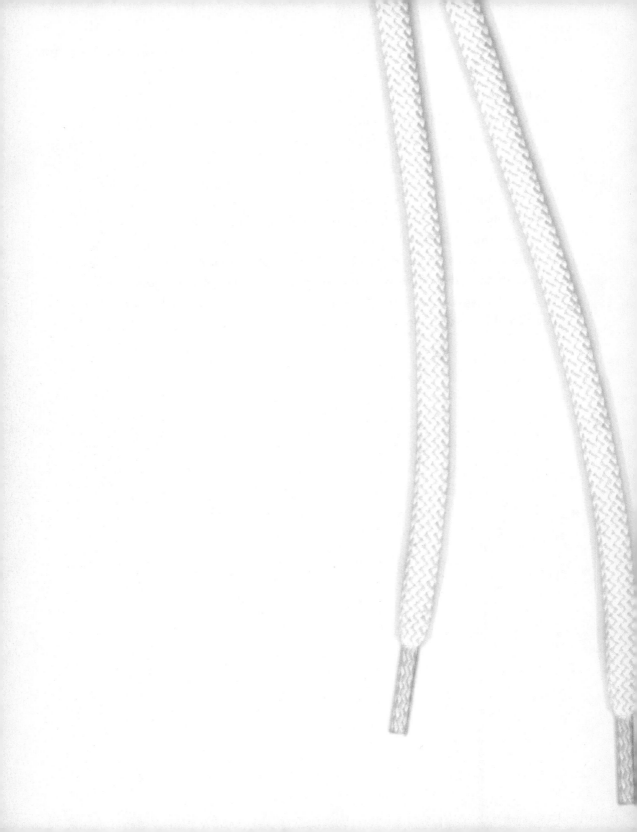

Part II:

The Tools

Chapter 6

Content Management on a Tight Budget

Chapter Checklist

1. **What do you really need?**

   Take the time to discover what you really need CMS to do; don't pay for solutions to problems you don't have.

2. **Does your CMS selection work with the tech skills you have on staff?**

   Make sure that as you select a CMS, you have a good inventory of what your technological expertise is. If you go for a system that requires tech skills that you do not have in-house, your investment will be wasted.

3. **Be creative.**

   Be creative about finding and tweaking tools available to you. Resources that are already at your disposal, such as server-side includes, might be enough solution for now. If you can save money by holding off on a CMS because you have a tool that works well enough, all the better.

4. **Do-it-yourself CMS.**

   Remember, too, that you can develop your own CMS. You might want to start small, creating a CMS that manages a boutique size site, and then move on to larger applications with more features. You will find that no CMS tool meets every one of your business needs, and you might spend time modifying any CMS you invest in. If you can't find a CMS that does exactly what you need, you might just want to develop your own system.

5. **Automate as much as you can.**

   CMS can save expensive admin time. Try to analyze how much mental and administrative work you do trying to manage a site, and think about how a CMS could save you money. If you have a labor-intensive, manual version-control system, you might be wasting money that a CMS could help you save.

6. **Consider open-source CMS.**

   Open-source CMS tools can be had for free (or for not much money) under an open-source license and can save you big bucks. If you select an open-source option, make sure that it has an active developer community, that your developers (that might be you!) like working with it, and that the application can scale as your site grows.

❝❝Here form is content, content is form.❞ ❞

—Samuel Beckett speaking of *Finnegan's Wake*.

As previous chapters have shown and as you know from your own experience, we shoestring web professionals have it tough. Our budgets don't allow for major mistakes or give us weeks of "creative" time to experiment with different design approaches. Luxuries such as original photography and vast font collections are typically beyond our grasp. We can't afford detailed usability studies, and we might not have a complete range of computing platforms and devices on which to test our work. After pestering our colleagues until they finally supply the content—or writing it ourselves—we often also do our own copy editing, proofreading, and text chunking.

But our problems don't end when the site goes live. They are just beginning. As additional content is written for the site, it is up to us to make the changes by hand. It is not uncommon for a shoestring web designer to respond to updated content or slightly modified site architecture by manually editing every single page on the site. Not only is this work tedious, but it is also expensive, eating otherwise billable hours each time the site is improved. As shoestring web professionals, we often can't afford to put in the hours required. All too frequently, the result is that site updates are late or don't get done at all. There has to be a better way to manage and maintain shoestring sites.

Content-Management Systems

Content management might provide the solution. *CMS*, which stands for content-management system, is an industry buzzword used to describe a wide range of tools. The term CMS covers expensive applications that manage every aspect of web content creation, publication, and maintenance. But CMS is also used to describe comparatively inexpensive (and even free) publishing tools that do little else than write chunks of text into otherwise static HTML pages.

Nearly all sites can benefit from some degree of automation in web publishing. Updating content consumes enough of your time, let alone needing to make changes by hand. A good CMS can empower you to work smarter, faster, and more logically.

Those kinds of benefits usually come at a high price. But as this chapter shows, there are many ways shoestring designers can save money while automating content management.

CMS does not magically solve every problem. If the system you buy or put together is not well matched to your needs, it might create as many dilemmas as it solves. To avoid CMS troubles, before you put your system together, take time to analyze what you need—and what you don't need. A few years ago, I managed the web site for The Branch Libraries of The New York Public Library. It was, and still is, a large site made up of smaller "satellite" sites. Each of these satellites was dedicated to a particular topic or service. Each had its own supervisor or team responsible for the freshness and accuracy of content on a certain part of the site. The setup might sound familiar to you. Many large public sector sites are organized in this way.

One of these sections required an update, and the people in charge of it spent hours editing the content. Unfortunately, instead of working off the most recent version, they updated text that was two or three versions old. Then they handed it off to my group, to be manually produced and installed on the site. We quickly discovered the error. Instead of simply producing the material, we were going to have to rewrite the rewrite. Proper version control, a tool that is sometimes part of a CMS, would have prevented the problem.

A version-control system tracks files and their authors. It is designed to prevent two authors from working on the same file at the same time, to avoid wasted hours editing the wrong version of a document, and to prevent other problems that crop up when many people work on the same project.

You might remember that, at the beginning of this book, I described how the Library had suddenly lost funding, preventing us from purchasing tools we thought we needed. A large CMS was one of these tools we had almost bought and then had not been able to afford. This particular CMS was a powerful content-management system, with a price tag to match—about $300,000, plus training and other professional services—which put it well beyond the reach of the shoestring professional. The CMS would have included advanced version control that would have prevented the editing error that we now had to solve manually.

But would this solution have been worth it? Think about that $300,000 price tag. Solving this particular version-control problem took us about six hours scattered over three days. We had one staff member compare each version of the site, making sure that all of the content was up-to-date. Let's assume that with that employee's salary and fringe benefits, the fix cost the organization $50 per hour. That brings the total cost to $300.

Certainly, manually fixing a problem that should not have happened in the first place was not good use of time and money. But did this waste of $300 justify the purchase of a $300,000 CMS? Hardly. Such a system might be the perfect product for those who can afford it, but it was *too much solution* for our small problem.

> ### Budget Threat
>
> It is easy to pay too much for a content-management system when you have not taken the time to know exactly what you want a CMS to do. Taking the time to define your needs and to explore make-shift alternatives that might already be at hand can save the shoestring web professional big bucks on CMS.

You might wonder why I cite such an expensive CMS product in my example. I do it because this little story illustrates the three greatest CMS threats to a shoestring budget:

- Not knowing what you need
- Paying for too much solution to your problem
- Not knowing what CMS-like tools you already have at your disposal

The trick on saving money on CMS is knowing exactly what your problems are— and *what they are not*—before you buy.

If you are on a shoestring budget, careful planning can help you identify your needs so that you get just the right solution and do not pay for *too much* solution.

Don't Pay for What You Don't Need

In addition to knowing what your content-management needs are, a question that is almost as important is, "What *don't* you need?" The potential to waste money on CMS is high when you have not given careful consideration to what you need and what you don't need. I have the same problem when I go shopping, especially in computer stores. I am easily tempted by the latest gadgets, finding that they provide solutions to problems I didn't know I had. For example, I did not know that I needed an Apple iPod until I saw one in a store. The informed consumer has a pretty good idea of what she really needs (and doesn't). The informed consumer on a budget stays focused on what she needs (for instance, a monitor when hers is broken) and doesn't blow the wad on things that are cool but not urgently required. So before going shopping, let's see what your needs might be.

Do You Need to Control Page Layout with Templates?

The most basic feature of a CMS is the capability to template a site. With templates, you can lock down certain areas of a web page, such as navigation and the logo area, leaving them uneditable except by certain personnel so that nontechnical content creators can't accidentally mess them up. Site managers and designers, obviously, can edit the locked-down areas so that they can update the site navigation or change the logo. Content specialists can edit only those page sections that are appropriate to their jobs. Simply put, templates allow you to administratively separate different chunks of your web pages (see Figures 6.1 and 6.2).

Page templates can be created a number of different ways, and you might not need a CMS to do this for you. As a good shoestring alternative, consider an HTML editor that provides template tools, such as with Macromedia Dreamweaver and Macromedia Contribute. It is possible to set up a template-driven site with such software and never need to spend a dime on a true CMS. It is important to note that Macromedia Dreamweaver and Contribute are desktop solutions for basic content-management problems. The savings come if you are already using this software for other purposes. Many CMS tools offer web-based administration of site content and settings; Contribute does this as well. This can be valuable to those on a limited budget because the only piece of software that the content author needs is a web browser. We look at several examples of web-based CMS later.

6.1 *The home page of The Picture Collection, a searchable database of images from one branch in The New York Public Library, as it appears to visitors (*`http://digital.nypl.org`*).*

6.2 *The template for this site allows only the dark gray content area to be edited by content contributors. The ghosted-out areas (in light gray) on the screen are parts of the template that only the site owner can edit. If there is a content update, the content author can work within the templated area that she or he has access to. If the logo or site navigation must change, only the site owner can change the template.*

Another non–CMS solution to templates is to use a free technology called *server-side includes*, or *SSI*. This might sound tricky, but it is not. Many web developers manage pages by leaving navigation and branding material in a separate web document that lives in its own file on the server but renders as a part of the web page when the site is displayed on a browser. Don't get it? Don't worry; we'll walk through an example. In the meantime, believe me when I tell you that server-side includes offer developers the economical capability to manage one set of "include" files for logo and navigation areas separately from the content portion of a web page (see Figure 6.3). Using SSI is sometimes all the automation many smaller sites need.

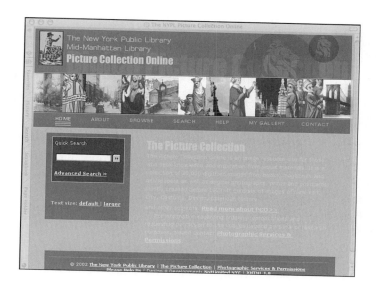

6.3 *The templates for this particular site are not managed with a proper CMS, but with server-side includes (SSI). Casually called "includes," SSI are files that sit independently from content pages on the server. The three dark gray areas, the top navigation, the left navigation, and the bottom navigation, are all different files that the main HTML page pulls in by using server-side includes.*

Definition: Server-Side Include

The term *server-side include (SSI)* covers a lot of ground. Most generally, an SSI is an HTML comment that tells the web server to dynamically populate a web page with content external to that page. That external content is maintained in a separate HTML page, much like a CSS or JavaScript document lives separately from the page or pages on which it is used. An SSI can populate a web page with a line of text or a chunk of data, or it can even execute a program. For instance, to take a basic example, an SSI can execute a small program that looks up the day, date, and time, and it can then insert that information into the HTML page. For our purposes, an SSI is an HTML comment that tells the server to pull the content from another HTML document.

One of the hallmarks of a successful shoestring site is that it takes advantage of the resources at hand; leveraging your server's capability to execute SSI can be the perfect way to do just that. If your site is small and is managed by only a few web professionals, SSI might be all you need to manage a site's various chunks of content. Refer to Figure 6.3 to learn more.

The following is the markup for the home page of The Picture Collection. Notice that it contains only the content that is specific to that particular page. The navigational and branding elements are in includes in Lines 2, 3, 4, and 19 (highlighted in bold). Remember that the way you write includes will vary from server to server. Ask your systems administrator for the proper syntax.

```
1.  <body>
2.  <!--#include virtual="/mainnav.txt" -->
3.  <!--#include virtual="/subnav.txt" -->
4.  <!--#include virtual="/search.txt -->
5.  <h1>The Picture Collection</h1>
6.  <p>The Picture Collection Online is an image resource
7.  site for those who seek knowledge and inspiration from
8.  visual materials. It is a collection of 30,000 digitized
9.  images from books, magazines and newspapers as well as
10. original photographs, prints and postcards, mostly created
11. before 1923. It consists of images of New York City,
12. Costume, Design, American History and other subjects. <a
13. href="about.cfm">Read more about PCO</a>.</p>
14. <p>For information regarding ordering reproductions and
15. requesting permission to use images beyond personal or
16. research purposes, please contact <a
17. href="http://www.nypl.org/admin/pro/copies/cs.html">
18. Photographic Services and Permissions</a>.</p>
19. <!--#include virtual="/footer.txt" -->
20. </body>
```

Do You Need Authoring and Editing Features?

A wonderful feature found in some CMS systems is an easy-to-use interface for authoring and editing content. Some CMS interfaces look much like word-processing software; others, such as Zope (see Figure 6.5), require HTML authoring experience. You might need an interface that is easy for nontechnical content authors to use. Do not rule out this kind of feature just because you are on a shoestring budget. You might find an affordable tool that meets this requirement. Take the time to list the features that you will need:

- Spell-checking utility
- WYSIWYG interface that allows nontechnical people to enter content without having to use or understand HTML (see Figures 6.4 and 6.5)
- Undo and redo capabilities
- Copy and paste support
- Capability to manually or automatically create metadata (see sidebar)
- Page formatting capability within your template
- Image placement control
- Required content areas (such as alternate text for images)

Definition: Metadata

Metadata is data about data. Metadata can be used in many different settings and for many different purposes. For our purposes, metadata describes the content and purpose of your web page. Many search engines use the metadata that you create as the description for your site, so there is significant value in creating this information. Here is the metadata for a real-live duct tape fashion site (www.ducttapefashion.com/):

```
<title>Duct Tape Clothing, fashion, wallets, hats, purses, and more! Duct Tape
Fashion Clothing and Accessories, and More!</title>
<meta name="DESCRIPTION" content="Duct Tape hats shoes backpacks dresses and
more! Showcased on TV, heard on RADIO, and read in 'News of the Weird'!">
<meta name="KEYWORDS" content="duct tape, duck tape, duct tape clothing, duct
tape accessories, cool gifts, unique gifts, weird, I've got a Secret,">
<meta name="author" content="Keith Drone">
```

Notice that there is a line of metadata for every bit of data about the site, including a title for the site, a description of the site, keywords that users might search on to find a site like this (okay, well, *some* users might search for a site like this), and author information.

Duct Tape Clothing, fashion, wallets, hats, purses, and more! ...
Duct Tape hats shoes backpacks dresses and more! ... Cheap! **Duct Tape** Book Only $5 Get
them while they last! Random **Duct Tape** Use of the Moment. Submit yours today! ...
Description: **Duct tape** wallets, purses, adjustable belts, hats and straps. Keith Drone's creations are unique.
Category: Shopping > Clothing > Accessories
www.ducttapefashion.com/ - 15k - Mar 28, 2003 - Cached - Similar pages

6.4 *When the Duct Tape Clothing site comes up in Google (shown here) or another search engine, the metadata displays in search results. Good shoestring web professionals leverage metadata to improve their display in such search engines rather than letting the search engine display random text from the body of the site.*

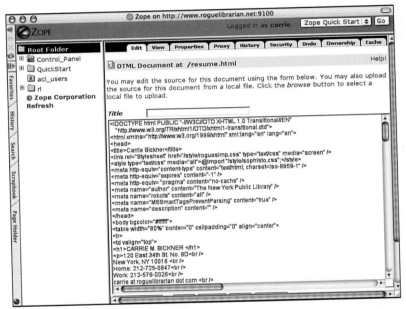

6.5 *If a graphical interface is one of your CMS requirements, the off-the-shelf configuration of Zope, an open-source CMS tool (www.zope.org), might not fit your bill immediately. To use Zope it its unaltered form, the content author needs to be able to write markup. However, as you'll see later, Zope can be modified so that it has an easy-to-use graphical interface. Note also that Zope allows users to upload HTML pages that can be authored in just about any HTML editor the user desires.*

Do You Need XHTML and CSS Support?

In Chapter 7, "Save Time and Money with Web Standards," we discuss the value of good markup and the savings you can enjoy with CSS. Assuming that I make a convincing enough case that well-constructed XHTML and CSS will save you money, you will probably want to make sure that the CMS you pick supports XHTML and CSS.

One of the things that you turn over to a CMS is authorship of markup; you set up a site, but the CMS produces much of the markup for the content. Not all types of CMS handle markup equally. Some systems do it rather deftly, writing elegant, accessible, standards-compliant XHTML. Other systems vomit out markup that is no better than the stuff authored by the worst HTML editors.

As you'll see in Chapter 7, there is considerable value in lean, nicely formed markup; your site is smaller and is less expensive in terms of bandwidth and storage. Your site is also accessible to a wider variety of users, including those on assistive technology and other nontraditional Internet devices, including PDAs.

As you gather your requirements, consider the savings you might enjoy from a site with good markup.

Do You Need Content Versioning and Workflow Management?

The version-control example that I gave in the introduction of this chapter is one kind of problem that can be solved with a CMS. We had no mechanism for keeping track of versions of a page or component, nor did we have the capability to roll back to an earlier version of a given page or component, or even an earlier version of the entire site. A CMS with real versioning and workflow-management capabilities will keep track of versions for you and will control the flow of the editorial process.

If your version problems are few because your staff is small and communicates well, site versioning might be overkill. However, you might have to pay for hidden labor costs if you do not have a tool that automates version control and workflow management. Do your developers have to download their entire directory every night before they go home? Are they shouting over cubicle walls, "Grace, stay out of the *about* directory for about an hour; I am working in there now."

The cost of these human interactions can add up in ways that you can't readily see. Assume that Grace is the kind of developer who works best when she listens to Taiwanese pop music with her headphones. Her colleagues make trips to her cubicle, tap her on the shoulder, and wait for her to remove the headphones to tell her not to work on a particular part of the site. Over the course of a year, the time wasted on these interactions is money down the toilet. A simple CMS with check-in and check-out functionality could allow Grace to work happily with her music and save some big bucks for the team. (With check-in and check-out functionality, as one professional grabs hold of a file or directory, others are locked out of it until the first professional has finished her task and "checked" the file back into the system.)

If you have more than two or three people working on a site, you can save significant labor costs with a check-in/check-out tool or with other version-management features. If your team is small, you might want to avoid paying for unnecessary features.

Do You Need Database Connectivity?

Most content-management systems connect to a database; in these cases, the database stores the content in its various versions. If your CMS requires a database, find out if a database comes with the package you are considering. Remember that the database purchase might be separate from your CMS investment. Many open-source (free and freely licensed) CMS tools can be used with open-source databases. We discuss these free options in the upcoming section "Open-Source CMS." Often your IT department or host will have one or two databases, already installed. If your CMS requires a database, make sure it will work with the database you have.

Do You Need Staging and Production Areas?

Many web professionals work on more than one server or work area as a means of managing different production and development tasks. A simple example of this kind of administration might look like this:

	Content
Development or Staging Area	Content creation and review
Production Area	Live content

In this scenario, there are two work areas, one for the creation and editing of content and another for live content. After the content is created and edited, it is promoted to the production area. Some content-management systems will automate that promotion for you. For example, the CMS might allow a content creator to push content to the development area with the click of a button. Then an editor works in that same development area to review the new content. When the editor is done, she can push the content to the production area, again with the click of a button. After she has done this, the content is live and on the web.

Another more complicated system of using staging and production areas occurs when you are developing software along with content. Let's say that you have an engineering team developing some chat software. At the same time, content creators are working on copy. You might want to manage the software development in the same way that you managed content creation in the previous example, by setting up a separate development area for building, testing, and debugging. When the chat software is ready to release, you can promote it to the production area.

If content creation is happening at the same time, you might want to keep that activity separate from the software development. In such a case, your staging and production areas will look like this:

	Software	Content or Data
Development or Staging Area	Software developed and tested	Content creation and review
Production Area	Live software	Live content

Staging and production areas can be broken apart in other ways. For some projects, one staging area might be for data, and another might be for web pages. Some CMS tools enable you to work across these staging and production areas, automating the process of promoting content from development to production. Remember that a CMS tool does not cover the cost of the various areas—it only provides the capability to work across those areas.

Even if you are not working in an environment like this now, you might be some day. If this looks like your future, consider what a messy and expensive process it is to move files from one area to another, and decide whether you want a CMS tool that helps you move from development to production.

Do You Need an RSS Feed?

Rich Site Summary (RSS) is an XML format that enables you to share web content. Don't worry—you are not going to have to do XML markup. For our purposes, RSS is a tool that gives you the capability to syndicate some portion of your web content (see Figure 6.6). An RSS feed enables users, including other web developers, to pick up and redistribute whatever you syndicate.

6.6 *Moreover (*`www.moreover.com`*) is an information brokerage firm that uses the RSS feeds that news sources provide. SiliconValley.com, Wired News, and The Registrar are all sites that provide RSS feeds; they have been picked up by Moreover. The potential to generate traffic based on your capability to syndicate your content this way is high. If you are in the business of providing content, you might seriously consider RSS. When contemplating an RSS strategy, think about CMS tools that generate one or more RSS feeds for you.*

Some users keep their own RSS watch list and visit sites when their RSS syndication indicates that a site has been updated. Many others rely on free (or inexpensive) News Reader software to display the new and changed RSS headlines and text from sites to which they have subscribed. (Subscription is free; you tell your News Reader which sites' RSS feeds you want to track by typing the URL of the site's RSS feed into a dialog box in the News Reader software. For instance, `www.scripting.com/`

`rss.xml` is one of the RSS feeds from the Scripting News web site.) News Readers visit sites that "aggregate" RSS feeds and then download the feeds you've subscribed to.

The benefit of having an RSS feed is that it is an inexpensive way to distribute your content more broadly and to generate site traffic. If you give users multiple opportunities to find out that your site has been updated, you give them more chances and more reasons to decide to come visit you again.

Spinning Straw into Gold: Email Newsletters

Many sites reach out to their community via newsletters (see Figure 6.7). This can be a cost-effective marketing tool; the capability to generate more traffic with a weekly newsletter should not be underestimated. I used to manage the JavaScript site on about.com, and I sent out newsletters once every two weeks. Site visits nearly doubled on the days following the newsletters' release. Net Words' Nick Usborne tells a similar story and has a tip for shoe-string publishers who want to make the most of their newsletters (see quote on next page):

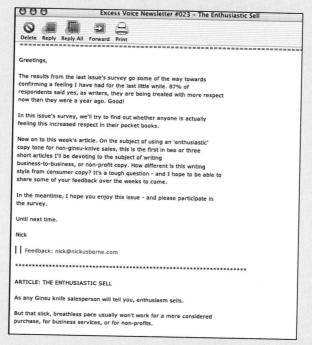

6.7 An email newsletter can generate a surprising amount of traffic to a site. You can create content for your site on a regular basis that could be repurposed in newsletter form. If this seems like a fit, consider the need for a tool to support automated (or streamlined) newsletter production when you go CMS shopping.

"I'm always surprised by the amount of activity generated by each newsletter I send out. I don't use the newsletter to sell—at least, not overtly. But each issue results in a flood of new visitors to my site. And if there is real value in your content, newsletters can be wonderfully viral. They get shared and forwarded to other people who would otherwise never have heard of you.

"Here is one of the most valuable lines of text in each issue of my own newsletter: Tell a friend or colleague about this newsletter...www.nickusborne.com/friend_excessvoice.htm."

The Best CMS for Your Buck

Now that you have listed some of the things that CMS can do for you, it is time to start shopping. Before you can determine the best CMS value for your small budget, you need to do three things:

1. **Gather your functional requirements.** Base this on the list of features described in the preceding section.

2. **Determine your budget.** Remember that this number has to cover not just the purchase of a CMS, but the entire investment. The investment might include training, professional services, and the cost to import legacy content. Additional investments might include hosting, add-ons, upgrades, support contracts, and other maintenance contracts. Balance these costs against the money you'll save in person hours over the short and long term.

Budget Threat

The cost of a CMS is not limited to the sticker price on the software itself. Sometimes a new CMS requires additional professional services for setup and for loading your old content into the new system. Further costs might come in the form of additional staff members with technical skills required to run the new system, or from auxiliary purchases such as extra servers, databases, or software licenses. Be sure to include all related costs before you select a CMS.

3. **Make sure to take an accurate inventory of the technical expertise you have on staff.** Be conservative; list only the expertise you anticipate retaining over the long haul. If you have only one or two technical people on staff and you can't predict their long-term commitment to the organization, let that uncertainty inform your CMS decision. (Plan for the worst-case scenario, and you might avoid living it.) Additionally, you might want to underestimate the *level* of expertise that you have on staff; this will keep you from having to foot the bill for a consultant when you find that your tech people are in over their

heads. As an example, if there is one overworked technical person on your staff whose skill in some areas is questionable and who has recently told you he is looking for another job, you might not want to choose an open-source CMS that requires technical knowledge to install and maintain.

I am an organized girl, and when I plan, I like to make charts. This helps me keep all of the decision-making factors in once place. In planning to make a CMS investment, I would make sure to list all of the features that I need, my technical requirements, and, of course, my budget.

Doing the same thing might help you move a decision forward. If you do not have control over your budget and need to get approval from above, having your thinking listed clearly and carefully will help your case. I would put my three CMS decision factors in a spreadsheet like the following.

Features Needed?	Answer	Notes
Do you need to control page layout with templates?	Yes	We do need to control site layout with templates. Editing our top navigation bar is a protracted task now; to change one link or image under the current system, we have to edit 20 different files. This is too time-consuming and creates too many opportunities for error.
Do you need authoring and editing features?	Somewhat	This is not critical yet, but as more nontechnical people begin to add content to the site, they will certainly need a simple interface to help them do that. If we can get this feature now, we'll have an easier transition when these nontech people join the project.
Do you need XHTML and CSS support?	Yes	We have made a highly public commitment to authoring good (X)HTML and CSS; now we need to put our money where our mouth is.
Do you need database connectivity?	Yes	We need our CMS to work with MySQL, the database that recently became our standard.
Do you need staging and production areas?	Maybe	This would be nice, but we will not need this for another two or three years. We might want to hold off on this if we can't have everything we want.
Do you need an RSS feed?	Yes	Our competitors have been using an RSS feed for about eight months, and reports indicate that they are generating quite a bit of traffic with this feature.

continues

Ideal for staff of 7 to 10	Very much	We have been working with some okay make-shift techniques for managing web development. For example, Dreamweaver's check-in/check-out tool helped us keep track of who was working on what. Now that our team has grown from three to seven, we need more serious file-management tools.
Versioning	Somewhat	It might be good if we can find a CMS that can help us with versioning, but if an affordable CMS meets our other requirements well enough, we can probably find a separate, inexpensive product for versioning.
Functional Requirements		
Runs on UNIX	Very much	This is our company's standard, and we can't afford to take on the cost of managing a new operating system. We have UNIX people on staff, but no one who has the skills to manage another OS.
Works with MySQL database	Very much	MySQL is our new standard. Remember that we must also support legacy MS Access databases for the next two years.
Easy to install and maintain	Very much	Our IT team is excellent, but it is overworked. We might have to do the installation ourselves, using IT's support only as a backup.
Other Factors		
Total budget	$10,000	This needs to cover our entire investment, training, support, and installation.
Skills on staff	PHP/Perl	
	XML/XSLT	
	Graphic design	
	(X)HTML and CSS	
	Apache/UNIX	
	SQL	
	MySQL, Access	We can work with other databases, but we need to limit our CMS to only those systems that work with our new standard, MySQL.

Now that you have your list of needed items and their importance, it's time to go shopping for an actual CMS. Let's review several options that I have selected from the broad categories of solutions that are on the market. For each category, I will highlight several CMS bargains, and then provide a detailed value study of one CMS in that group. Please do not assume that my main example is the best example or best product; you really need to do your own homework. Just use these examples as an intellectual exercise that will help you make the best decision. Be sure to follow up on the other CMS products listed and to extend your research to include even CMS systems that I have not mentioned. By the time this book is published, there are sure to be new products on the market.

Open-Source CMS

Definition time: Open-source software is software that is distributed under an open-source license. In most cases, the idea is that the software can be compiled, used, redistributed, and modified by anyone who so desires, as long as that person is working within the terms of the license for that software. The principle behind the open-software movement is that if software can be freely distributed and modified by members of an open-source community, that software will improve over time, at a fraction of the cost of proprietary products (or at no cost).

The open-source Linux operating system is one of the most famous (and successful) examples of the movement. The free, scalable PHP server-side language used on hundreds of thousands of web sites (including Yahoo.com) is another.

Not all open-source products are free. Open Office is an open-source office productivity suite that competes with Microsoft Office and runs in Linux, UNIX, Windows, and Mac OS. It costs much less than Microsoft Office but does not do everything MS Office can do (nor does it claim to).

When a piece of software is "open-sourced," its original developers create a public license that delineates the terms of use for that software. If the software takes off, a developer community begins to emerge. Members of that community start to modify and extend the original software, improving and expanding it over time. This has happened with Linux, Apache, PHP, Mozilla, and KHTML (the open-source code that drives the Konqueror and Safari browsers). That most open-source software is free to use under open-source licenses makes such products highly attractive to those working on a shoestring budget.

There are as many flavors of open source software as there are commercial: word processors, server software, mail programs, web browsers, and, of course, content-management systems. For this chapter, we focus on open-source CMS.

Not all open-source products are of the same quality or carry the same kind of license, and you really have to be careful about how you select one. In fact, open-source CMS might not be for everyone. Despite their low (or nonexistent) purchase price, open-source products might represent a larger human resource investment because such products often require that at least one person on your team can install and modify the CMS.

As you consider an open-source CMS, and I strongly encourage you to consider it, look for these five characteristics of a winning open-source product:

1. **An active developer community.** The more active the community is, the more improvements and support will be available to you.

2. **Scalability.** Make sure that the CMS tool you are considering will scale to your business needs. Do not invest your time, energy, and, yes, money in a CMS that will not scale as your site grows. (As an example, the open-source PHP language scales to meet Yahoo!'s needs—that's a good sign.)

3. **Support.** You might need to hire a consultant as you begin to use an open-source CMS. Make sure that support is available in your area.

4. **Appeal to your programmers, developers, or you.** A proven indicator of the success of any new technology is its appeal to developers. If your programmers don't like it, they will not use it successfully.

5. **Meets your business needs.** Finally, you need to make sure that your business needs are truly met by the CMS you are considering. Do not waste time and money installing a CMS that does not offer the functionality that you need, and then dribble away more hours trying to make the best of a bad situation or retrofitting your business needs to justify a system that doesn't actually help you.

Just as you would expect in commercial open-source CMS, there is a whole range of CMS tools, from large-scale enterprise tools to small-scale applications. Let's start with the biggies, enterprise CMS.

Open-Source Enterprise CMS Solutions

An enterprise CMS is, simply put, one that will stand up to heavy business demands and large volumes of traffic. Think IBM, Microsoft, Amazon, Yahoo!, Apple, and Google. These are the big guns of web publishing, and they use the big guns of the CMS world. This section introduces you to the some of the best regarded open-source options in this class of CMS. We look at a several options; then we zero in on one system and use it as an example in measuring a CMS against the scale, traffic, and functionality requirements that come with the enterprise turf.

A CMS Bargain: Midgard

Our first example, Midgard, is not really a CMS, but a content-management framework (`www.midgard-project.org/`). If you are a developer, you might want to use Midgard as the framework of a CMS that you develop. Consumers normally turn to CMS systems such as Aegir, Asgard, and PHPmole that are built around the Midgard framework. Midgard is built on Apache, PHP, and MySQL components, and that fits in with the skill set we outlined earlier when discussing the technical savvy of staff members that is required to complement open-source products. Midgard's strengths lie in its good support for editorial workflow and approval mechanisms, and its capability to automatically attach metadata to all of your content.

A CMS Bargain: PHPmole

PHPmole uses Midgard as a framework but also has a nice development environment that includes a visual HTML editor and other easy-to-use graphical development tools. PHPmole, like many open-source projects, is a labor of love and is constantly evolving. If your office or organization relies heavily on MS Word for content creation, you might look at another Midgard-based CMS called Aegir CMS (`www.aegir-cms.org/`) (see Figure 6.8). Aegir also supports several language encodings, including Unicode. If you are writing content in such languages as Finnish, German, Chinese, Russian, or Maori, you might want to try this CMS because of its built-in language support.

When listing the functional requirements for a CMS in an earlier part of this chapter, easy installation was noted as a highly desired feature. OpenCMS (`www.opencms.com`) might fill the bill. OpenCMS comes with an HTML setup wizard that helps you connect to a database. It also comes with tools that help you manage workflow; this enables you to more easily administer and separate content creation, editing, and publication tasks, as discussed in the earlier chapter section "Do You Need Staging and Production Areas?" OpenCMS also comes with a visual editor so that nontechnical people can easily create and update content.

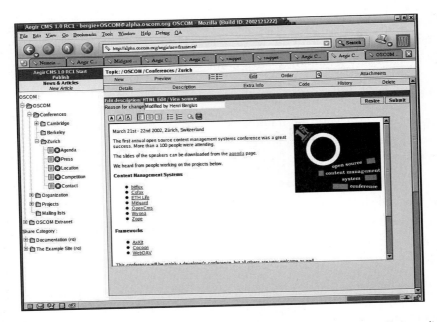

6.8 *Aegir (`www.aegir-cms.org/`) is freely available under an open-source license. It uses the well-regarded Midgard CMS framework at its core and offers some easy-to-use graphical interfaces such as that seen in this HTML editor. In the previous section on planning, we stated that a simple, web-based, visual interface like this would eventually be needed for the hypothetical project so that nontechnical content creators could work on the site easily. This interface would fulfill that functional requirement well.*

Value Study: Zope

Of the large-scale, enterprise CMS tools, Zope is among the most well known. I must also admit to a bias: I use Zope for one of my sites. Understand, therefore, that I selected it as the primary example of an open-source, enterprise CMS mainly because I know it the best.

Zope was one of the first open-source CMS tools to hit the scene; in 1998, the Zope Corporation released this software to open source. Zope also includes its own application server, which might be a value-added feature or a distraction, depending on how you see it. Zope comprises web and FTP server software that draws content from a database, such as Oracle, MySQL, or SQL Server 2000.

Platform and System Requirements

Zope runs on all major platforms, including Linux, Solaris, Windows, and Mac OS.

What Kind of Site It Is Best For

Zope was designed for enterprise sites. Current users include the U.S. Department of Agriculture, Viacom, AARP, the U.S. Navy, and NATO. But Zope can be effective on smaller sites. I use it to manage my personal site, Rogue Librarian, which is a one-person show comprising fewer than 300 pages. So don't assume that you're "too small" to benefit from Zope.

Support

You can receive support for free from Zope site Euro Zope (`www.eurozope.org/`) and email mailing lists. You can also pay for support from the Zope Corporation or many other companies that work with Zope.

Source

You can download Zope from `www.Zope.org/Products`.

Skills Required

You might discover a hidden cost in Zope when you have to hire talent to maintain the system. Most of Zope is written in the Python language, so you will need to have Python-capable talent on staff if you want to customize it—and, as we have discussed, most CMS needs to be customized. Python programmers are not as ubiquitous as other kinds of programmers, so you might face staffing challenges that you can't afford. But if your plans for implementation are not too ambitious, you can use Zope's off-the-shelf configuration and learn Python as you go, making small modifications when you need them. This approach, however, will not work if you are looking for an enterprise solution. Of course, you will need to be comfortable with whatever database you use as a back end.

Finally, it helps to be familiar with tag-based presentation and scripting languages. Zope uses the Document Template Markup Language (DTML) to automatically generate, control, and format content. DTML is the building block of the Zope system, so you will need to learn this language if you hope to do some of the fun stuff that a CMS lets you do. If you have some practice with tag-based presentation and scripting languages, such as ColdFusion, you will probably have an easy enough time picking up DTML. If you have little experience, you might want to play around with Zope before you commit to it. In this case, a good background in PHP indicates that you have the stuff to at least learn DTML.

Databases Supported

On UNIX, you can use Oracle, PostgreSQL, MySQL, Sybase, InterBase, and DB2. On Windows, you can use any ODBC-compliant database, including SQL Server 2000. For details, see `www.zopenewbies.net/faq.html`, question 2.11 ("Which databases can I use with Zope?").

Special Features

Zope Products are helper applications that you can use to add powerful, specific features to your site. Job listing boards, payment systems, enterprise portals, message boards, and calendars are just a few. For a comprehensive list of Zope Products, see The Zope Community Products list (`www.zope.org/Products`).

Zope Resources

One of the advantages of going with Zope is that it has an active development community. Resources to help you learn about the product are, in general, quite good. You will also find that there are many developers building small applications that extend Zope's capabilities. Here are a few resources to get you started:

- Zope Community (`www.zope.org/`)
- Zope Newbies (`www.zopenewbies.net/`)
- The Zope Book (`www.zope.org/Documentation/Books/ZopeBook/`)

Is Zope a Good Value?

Now that you have done a little research, it is time to update the planning spreadsheet that you started in a previous section of the chapter. Doing this will help determine whether Zope is a good value for your particular needs. Let's see how Zope fares.

Features Needed?	Answer	How Zope Measures Up
Do you need to control page layout with templates?	Very much	Zope enables us to create and manage templates quite easily.
Do you need authoring and editing features?	Somewhat	Zope doesn't do this without modification. An extension called IE Editor for Zope (http://vsbabu.org/webdev/zopedev/ieeditor.html) solves that problem.
Do you need XHTML and CSS support?	Very much	Zope supports this, if configured properly.
Do you need database connectivity?	Very much	Zope works with our standard, the MySQL database.
Do you need staging and production areas?	Not sure	Zope is configured to work across a staging and production area on the AARP web site. See the case study at www.zope.com/CaseStudies/aarp.
Do you need an RSS feed?	Very much	We can build one pretty easily. One approach is outlined in this article at XML.com, "Advanced XML Applications in Zope" (www.xml.com/pub/a/2000/02/23/zope/).
Ideal for staff of 7 to 10	Very much	Zope can also be used for a much larger team.
Versioning	Somewhat	Zope enables users to "check out" and "lock" documents so that only one person can work on a page at once. Zope also has a rollback tool that enables us to revert to an earlier version of any given page.
Functional Requirements		
Runs on UNIX	Very much	Zope works well on UNIX.
Works with MySQL database	Very much	This is not a problem with Zope.
Easy to install and maintain	Very much	This is so-so. (Some Zope sites suggest that it is quite easy to install. My impression is that these sites have a strong Zope bias. I have also read reports that indicate that Zope can be quite a bear to install.)

continues

Other Factors		
Total budget	$10,000	If we select Zope, our budget might go toward the cost of a vendor to install Zope and then for training so that we can learn how to extend Zope's capabilities.
Skills on staff	PHP/Perl	
	XML/XSLT	This might come in handy when we set up an RSS feed.
	Graphic design	
	(X)HTML and CSS	
	Apache/UNIX	
	SQL	
	MySQL	We can work with other databases, but we need to limit our CMS to only those systems that work with our new standard, MySQL.

Remember that you are working with a hypothetical budget of $10,000. Sure, Zope is free, but as you have just learned, it might not be that easy to install. You are also assuming that your in-house technical expertise is limited. A budget of $10,000 might be needed for the professional services required to get Zope up and running. A support contract might not be a bad idea, and that would cost a few bucks.

Because your budget is small, your functional requirements are rather easily (almost too easily) met by Zope, and you might spend your whole budget on support and training, you might wonder whether Zope is *too much solution* to your problem. You should consider some smaller-scale open-source CMS solutions and look at some inexpensive commercial systems as well.

Smaller-Scale Open-Source CMS

In the last section, you learned about the large-scale, open-source CMS. After evaluating the needs for your imaginary site, you found that an enterprise solution might be too much solution to your problem. So, let's look at a few small to midrange open-source systems and see if they fit the bill. Again, we consider a few bargains in brief and then investigate one Value Study, for the sake of continuing the exercise.

A CMS Bargain: Textpattern

Textpattern (www.textpattern.com/) is a new CMS developed by designer and developer Dean Allen. Textpattern is a good example of a simple CMS that does a few jobs well (see Figure 6.9). One of its strengths is that it has excellent support of (X)HTML and CSS; this was one of the requirements in the hypothetical needs list.

Textpattern enables you to set up an RSS feed and works with MySQL, so it meets some of the hypothetical site's needs. However, with only five predefined admin levels (see Figure 6.10), it might not be a powerful enough administrative tool.

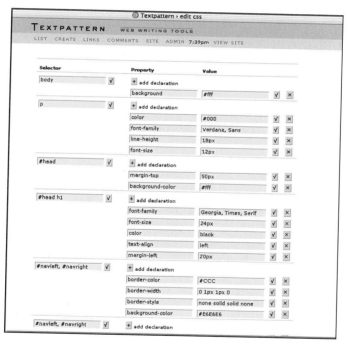

6.9 *Textpattern (www.textpattern.com/), a nifty new open-source CMS, enables you to set up and manage a CSS for your site. CSS is an economical way to manage and deliver a site's design. We cover the value of CSS in the next chapter.*

6.10 *Textpattern also enables you to assign varying levels of permission to different users. The administrative interface lets you set precise (and different) access levels for site publishers, managing editors, copy editors, authors, and designers.*

A CMS Bargain: Greymatter

More developed than Textpattern is Greymatter (`www.noahgrey.com/greysoft/`), which is specifically designed to handle journal or web log sites, although you might be able to tweak it for use in a different genre. Greymatter gives you the capability to add content to a site by sending an email message to your server; it also has automated RSS feed capability and a spell-check tool that you can add to the interface.

Value Study: Movable Type

One of the most interesting midsize open-source content-management systems to hit the scene is Movable Type. Let's see if this tool satisfies your requirements.

Platform and System Requirements

You need a web server that supports MySQL or the less well-known database Berkeley DB. Although it is little known in the design community, almost all hosting companies support Berkeley DB. You also need a server that enables you to run custom CGI scripts and that gives you least 25MB of free disk space. Software requirements change over time. See www.movabletype.org/requirements.shtml for the latest requirements and for information on how you can easily find out whether your hosting company supports the required technologies.

What Kind of Site It Is Best For

Movable Type is best for personal sites and journals that are updated regularly. Although the personal web log is the ideal site for Movable Type, this software can be tweaked to serve a variety of purposes (see Figure 6.11).

"Exploit Boston! Greater Boston's Independent Guide to Art, Culture, and Entertainment Events," a nonjournal, nonblog community site (www.exploitboston.com), uses Movable Type to run a calendar that groups events by category and date, and enables users to suggest events.

Support

Community members and the creators of the software populate Movable Type support forums.

Source

The distribution can be downloaded from the Movable Type web site at www.movabletype.org/download.shtml. The accompanying manual is also on the movabletype.org site at www.movabletype.org/docs/mtinstall.html.

Skills Required

If you are nontechnical, you might need help installing Movable Type on your server. When it is set, you can run it relatively trouble free. If you have experience programming in Perl, you can write custom dynamic applications using the Movable Type libraries; this enables you to add functionality to your site.

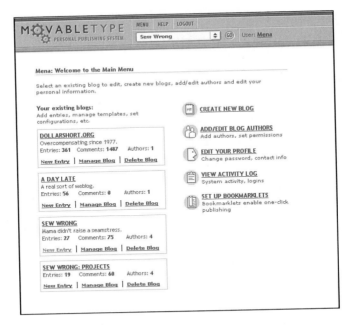

6.11 *The popular open-source CMS Movable Type requires at least basic knowledge of HTML for content creators and content editors.*

Special Features

These features include RSS feeds, a search engine, a built-in commenting system, an email notification system, entry categorization that "classifies" each entry for browsing, trackback (which facilitates cross-site connections), and a Hold/Release status that allows for content editorial and approval by setting entries to be placed on "hold" for editorial review and then "released" following approval.

Extensibility is one of Movable Type's greatest virtues. Like Zope and many other open-source CMS products, it benefits from third-party add-on applications that you can use to enhance your site. These add-ons include RSS calendar tools, web site categorization, a Smarty Pants module that generates typographically correct quotation marks and apostrophes, and other nifty things. The Movable Type development community is an active one, so expect to see more enhancements as time goes on.

Let's update the spreadsheet to see how Movable Type fits the $10,000 bill.

Features Needed?	Answer	How Movable Type Measures Up
Do you need to control page layout with templates?	Very much	Movable Type enables us to create and manage templates quite easily.
Do you need authoring and editing features?	Somewhat	Movable Type ships with only a simple interface for adding content, but there are several plug-ins that allow for graphical editing.
Do you need XHTML and CSS support?	Very much	Movable Type supports this, if configured properly.
Do you need database connectivity?	Very much	Movable Type works with our standard, the MySQL database.
Do you need staging and production areas?	Not sure	Movable Type does not support this.
Do you need an RSS feed?	Very much	Movable Type supports this easily.
Ideal for staff of 7 to 10	Very much	Movable Type is fine with a team of this size.
Versioning	Somewhat	This is not exactly supported, but Movable Type does have the capability to put new entries on hold for editorial review.
Functional Requirements		
Runs on UNIX	Very much	Movable Type works well on UNIX.
Works with MySQL database	Very much	This is not a problem.
Easy to install and maintain	Very much	Movable Type is much easier to install and maintain than Zope.
Other Factors		
Total budget	$10,000	Movable Type does much of what we are looking for and should not take up too much of our budget. The product is free for nonprofit or noncommercial use (although its creators request a donation of $20 or more if you are so inclined), and a commercial license costs a mere $150.
Skills on staff	PHP/Perl	
	XML/XSLT	
	Graphic design	
	(X)HTML and CSS	
	Apache/UNIX	
	SQL	
	MySQL	

Is Movable Type a Good Value?

Let's assume that the hypothetical site is not going to be a journal or web log; this means that you might be using Movable Type to do a job that is slightly different from what it was created for. However, Movable Type is powerful and flexible enough to manage different kinds of sites. Exploit Boston Type (`www.exploitboston.com/`) is a fine example of a nonblog site powered by Movable Type and supercharged by third-party Movable Type add-on modules. Figures 6.12–6.14 demonstrate how Exploit Boston uses some of the add-on calendar tools that are readily available.

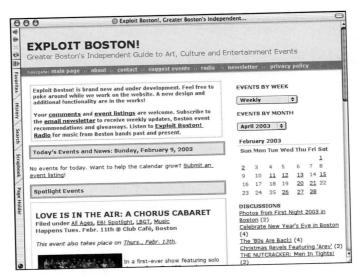

6.12 *Exploit Boston (www.exploitboston.com/), a site that is run on a lot of love and little money, is dedicated to culture and the arts in Beantown. The site's producer, Sooz Kaup, employs Movable Type, a CMS that is more typically used to manage web log–style personal sites, to maintain an online directory of events. But Kaup has created a success by taking advantage of free resources at hand.*

About the event ...

Title

Date (Click to Select Date)

Doors Open
hh:mm a/p

Start Time
hh:mm a/p

End Time
hh:mm a/p

Event website

Event logo/graphic
http://

Cost

Location Name/Venue

Location Street Address

Location City, State, Zip Code

Location website

6.13 *Movable Type is powerful enough for Kaup to provide a form enabling users to suggest events. This input is key to the success of a site with such volatile content. In her administrative interface, Kaup can review, edit, and publish those events that she chooses to include.*

EVENTS BY CATEGORY
18+
21+
All Ages
Art
Benefit
Crafts
Dance
EB! Announcements
EB! Photo Albums
EB! Spotlight
Festivals
Food and Drink
Free
Humor
LBGT
MBTA Green Line
MBTA Red Line
Movies
Music
New Year's Eve
Other
Poetry
Smokefree
Theater and Plays
Variety Show

UPDATES AND NEWS
Sign-up with your email address to receive Boston event recommendations, news and giveaways. (more info)

join

6.14 *Kaup has modified Movable Type in a way that maintains a fine-grain category system for events. Movable Type also enables user to opt in to an email notification list for future events.*

It will take work to make Movable Type perform as nonjournal software, but in this hypothetical example, you have the skills on staff to do it. Neither Zope nor Movable Type meets every last one of your needs here, but both fulfill the high-priority requirements, with one exception: Zope might fall short on ease of installation, and you will not know until you try whether it is easy enough for you. For that reason alone, you might want to try Movable Type first. If the transition is smooth, you might be able to save that $10,000 for something else, such as the office party fund.

Given that the development communities for both products are active, you are likely to see Zope and Movable Type grow. So if you go with Movable Type, you might one day see support for working across staging and production areas, and the capability to handle more complex versioning problems. You would have to make an educated guess on whether Movable Type will inevitably offer these features—and how important they are to your long-term needs.

But before you decide, you have more solutions to consider. If you limit yourself to open-source options, you make a long-term staffing commitment to managing the software. You'll need your own in-house people to keep up with new releases and to extend and maintain the application. You might be able to find consultants to do this work for you, but that would cost money, too.

Concerns about these long-term staffing investments are what cause many people to choose commercial systems. Look at a few of these commercial CMS products before you make a commitment.

Commercial CMS

Let's get the expensive stuff out of the way. At the high and midrange of commercial CMS, there are many systems to select from. Those with more money might choose from products such as Interwoven (`www.interwoven.com`) and BroadVision (`www.broadvision.com/`). These systems can cost hundreds of thousands of dollars. (Each CMS installation is unique to each company, so prices fluctuate.) The total investment for such a tool might be more when you add the cost of professional services that are required for installation, training, and legacy content importation. There are also many midrange CMS systems to select from, priced between $40,000 and

$100,000. These include Merant (`www.merant.com/`), Ingeniux (`www.ingeniux.com/`), Paperthin (`www.paperthin.com/`), and Mediasurface (`www.mediasurface.com/`).

I am going to assume that anyone holding this book is not interested in the midrange to high-end enterprise CMS solutions, but it is helpful to know just how much you can pay for the big guns. Now let's skip straight to the cheap ones. In keeping with the hypothetical constraints that we have been working with, we stick with systems that are much less than $10,000.

There are as many affordable commercial CMS solutions as there are stars in the heavens. Okay, there aren't that many, but there are some.

A CMS Bargain: WebWorld

WebWorld (`http://cms.webworld.biz/`) costs between $29 and $159 per user. WebWorld's role-based administration enables you to assign administrative, user, and guest accounts to your staff so that you can give each member of your team only the access level that enables everyone to do what they need. In addition to controlling WebWorld-generated pages, the product can update pages that were created by another company's CMS or even by hand. WebWorld also ships with a search engine that you can set up to include pages that were not created by the WebWorld CMS. That you can treat legacy content so easily might save you staff time: Rather than painfully migrating your old content into your new CMS, you can incorporate it rather easily in this way.

WebWorld has a browser-based WYSIWYG editor for creating and editing content, so nontechies can perform updates without having to understand a lick of HTML. They also can do their jobs from anywhere as long as they have MS Internet Explorer 5.0 or higher. Earlier in the chapter, I mentioned the value of web-based authoring. Some solutions require that users have a special piece of software installed on their personal computers; this means that you have to buy the software for each user and that you have to pay for the staff time to install that software. Web-based access to your CMS might therefore be a desirable feature for you. WebWorld is not unique in offering web-based access; many content-management systems work this way, including the low-cost and free web log-management packages that we looked at a few pages ago. But just because it is common doesn't mean that it is everywhere. If web access is important to you, make sure that the package you select has this option.

A CMS Bargain: AssetNow

If the names Microsoft and Macromedia mean a lot in your shop, AssetNow (www.assetnow.com/) might be what you are looking for. The commercial version of AssetNow costs between $1,000 and $2,500, depending on the license. There is also a free personal edition of the same tool that you can use for personal and non-commercial sites. If you are considering AssetNow, you might try the personal edition on a personal site first; this will give you a chance to become familiar with the basic structure of the tool. If you are happy, you can bring the commercial version to your day job.

The platform requirements for AssetNow are different from the open-source tools we were looking at. Instead of using PHP, this application uses Macromedia ColdFusion MX/5.0 application server. In addition to working on Linux, AssetNow runs on the Microsoft Windows NT/2000/XP operating system. And instead of open-source databases such as MySQL, AssetNow works with Microsoft Access.

The benefit of working with Access is that you probably already have it; you purchased it with MS Office. The trouble with Access is that it is not really up to the task of running busy, database-driven sites; it was developed to be a desktop application, not a web-based application. If you and your users conduct many web transactions—for example, if you are an e-commerce site—you do not have a good guarantee that your data will be secure. Also, if your site becomes popular, Access will not stand up to high traffic demands. If you are just getting started, you can develop your site with Access and then move to MySQL later; just don't wait too long, or you might find yourself vested in and stuck with a system that no longer meets your needs.

AssetNow might also be worthwhile if you are working on a small intranet application. If you have a limited number of users and you keep your databases simple, you should be fine. In addition, AssetNow offers good support for CSS and (X)HTML, so you can create well-constructed pages that are as easy on the bandwidth as they are on the eyes.

Definition: UNIX and Linux

UNIX is an operating system that was developed at Bell Labs in the early 1970s. Over the years, UNIX has evolved considerably and has become a popular operating system for universities. Linux is a newer version of UNIX and is a tremendously popular, freely available, open-source operating system developed mainly by a fellow named Linus Torvalds. Linux has extended the popularity of UNIX, and you will find that more people are using UNIX/Linux for not only servers, but for personal computers as well. The Macintosh OS X operating system is based on another flavor of UNIX and includes open-source tools and protocols behind the friendly Mac candy shell.

Definition: Intranet

An *intranet*, like the Internet, is a network of computers that shares information, but an intranet's network is private and self-contained. A company or organization's secure intranet is accessible only to members of that company or organization.

Value Study: Easy Publish

A Zope for the rest of us? Easy Publish is based on the free, open-source product Zope, discussed earlier in the chapter. Easy Publish might be easy, but it is not free. The reason that the cost (about $2,300) might be worth it is that Easy Publish assembles some of the add-on features that are available for Zope so you don't have to. In short, it is a labor saver—and time is money.

Platform

Easy Publish works on Windows 95/98/NT/2000 or Solaris, Linux, BSD, Mac OS X, and others.

What Kind of Site It Is Best For

Because this is a Zope-based product, you can use it for a large, high-traffic site. Of course, you can use Easy Publish on smaller sites as well, but if one of your requirements is that your CMS stands up to lots of traffic, Easy Publish will work for you. Some of Easy Publish's current customers include Cap Gemini Ernst & Young England, BioCentrum Technical University of Denmark, and The Danish Civil Aviation Administration.

Support

Easy Publish offers support contracts; prices vary. Technical support can be had for $35 for 15 minutes.

Source

See www.easypublisher.com to download Easy Publish.

Skills Required

As with Zope, Python might be handy, but what you get with Easy Publish is a product that works off the shelf.

Databases Supported

On UNIX, you can use Oracle, PostgreSQL, MySQL, Sybase, InterBase, and DB2. On Windows, you can use any ODBC-compliant database, including SQL Server 2000.

Special Features

The special features are about what you get with Zope, but Easy Publish has carefully assembled key Zope-based add-ons that you would have to find and install yourself if you were simply to use Zope.

Cost

A corporate license for Easy Publish, with an unlimited number of users, costs about $2,340. Individual, noncommercial licenses are available for free.

Features Needed?	Answer	How Easy Publish Measures Up
Do you need to control page layout with templates?	Very much	Just like Zope, Easy Publish enables us to create and manage templates quite easily.
Do you need authoring and editing features?	Somewhat	Whereas Zope required modification, Easy Publish has built this feature into the CMS: It sports WYSIWYG editing with support for typographic styles, link dialog, image dialog, accelerators, undo, bulleted lists, and numbered lists.
Do you need XHTML and CSS support?	Very much	Easy Publish supports this if page templates are set up correctly.
Do you need database connectivity?	Very much	Easy Publish works with our standard, the MySQL database.
Do you need staging and production areas?	Not sure	Staging and version support is available as an add-on; we would pay for additional consulting services. It ships with workflow and publishing modules that notify users when they have something to edit or publish.
Do you need an RSS feed?	Very much	As with Zope, we can build one pretty easily. If Easy Publish does not ship with RSS, we can modify Easy Publish or pay for a consultant to modify Easy Publish to add an RSS feed.
Ideal for staff of 7 to 10	Very much	Easy Publish can also be used for a much larger team.
Versioning	Somewhat	Easy Publish enables users to "check out" and "lock" documents so that only one person can work on a page at once. Easy Publish also has a rollback tool that enables us to revert to an earlier version of any given page.
Functional Requirements		
Runs on UNIX	Very much	Easy Publish works well on UNIX.
Works with MySQL database	Very much	This is not a problem.
Easy to install and maintain	Very much	This would be part of the professional services that we buy when we license the product.
Other Factors		
Total budget	$10,000	Cost is $2,340 plus professional services. We need to get a quote for installation and support.
Skills on staff	PHP/Perl	
	XML/XSLT	
	Graphic design	
	(X)HTML and CSS	
	Apache/UNIX	
	SQL	
	MySQL	We can work with other databases, but we need to limit our CMS to only those systems that work with our new standard, MySQL.

Not Really CMS

One other resource should be considered as you look at content-management solutions, but this is not really CMS. It is actually a scaled-back, visual web page editor by Macromedia. Contribute is the name of the product, and it costs $100 a pop. You get a lot of bang for those bucks. (But remember that Contribute is a desktop application, not a web-based application, so each user must pay for and install the software on his or her own computer.)

You can give Contribute to a nontechnical web author, and the graphical interface enables that person to edit web pages easily. When someone publishes a page after working on it, that person is actually using an FTP client built into the software. As with full-fledged CMS systems, administrators decide which parts of which pages each user can edit. Contribute does not have the capability to interact with databases, so this is a solution that involves static pages. However, you can create templates with server-side includes or Dreamweaver templates. And unlike some CMS products, Contribute lets users "roll back" to a previous page version.

Last but Not Least

Finally, I'd like to share one tip I didn't cover in the chapter:

Do not spend money on multiple outputs of a single page.

There is no need to pay for software that manages multiple outputs of content. Some CMS vendors will sell you on the capability to output for various web browsers, PDAs, and other devices. As you'll see in the next chapter, though, this is a waste because web standards make it easy to build a site one time, one way, and have it work well on a wide variety of devices. Take a breather to reward yourself for getting through this chapter, and then join me in the next one as we explore the perfect marriage between web standards and shoestring budgets.

Chapter 7

Save Time and Money with Web Standards

Chapter Checklist

1. **If you are on a limited budget, make sure that you invest some of your time and money on creating a standards-compliant site.**

   This will pay off as you build the site, and even more as you maintain it.

2. **Remember the value of keeping separation between structure and presentation.**

   When it comes time to redesign your site, the XHTML structure should not have to be altered. You might need to add a few special divisions, identifiers, or classes, but the basic structure should hold from one design version to the next. Reworking the presentation of a site should ideally be limited to altering the style sheets.

3. **Build one site, and build it well.**

   If you use well-structured markup, you should never have to create and maintain multiple versions of your site. One good site will work equally well on traditional browsers, handheld devices, and assistive technology. Be user agent–agnostic, and all users will love you for it.

4. **Remember that CSS is a much more powerful design tool than presentational HTML ever hoped to be.**

   You can control margins, leading, and typography, as well as create rollovers and other interactive effects. All of this can be had with just a few lines of CSS—a shoestring bargain if there ever was one.

" To do good work, one must first have good tools. "

—Chinese proverb

How Web Standards Help You Save

One of my great grandmothers went dotty in her last years. Fearful that people would "get" her money, she removed the cash from her savings account and literally burned it in her two-slice toaster. Web sites do the same thing every day when they use outdated markup and coding techniques. No site can really afford this, shoestring sites least of all. Used well, web standards can protect you from burning through your budget.

At a recent design conference, noted web standards evangelist Eric Meyer (author of *Eric Meyer on CSS*, New Riders Publishing, 2002) spoke about a well-known, heavily used e-commerce web site that wastes about a terabyte of bandwidth transfers per year, lowering the site's response time and making transactions slower—thus risking customer loss simply because of the way the site's left navigation menu is marked up.

Rather than using a simple, valid HTML list styled with CSS, the site keeps each menu item in a table cell with a spacer GIF and a little blue GIF arrow. Given that the menu is about 50 items long, the cost of serving each blue arrow is quite expensive.

Meyer noted that if the site were to simplify the menu's markup and point to the blue arrow with a CSS style rather than with a table cell for each menu item, the site's owners could bring the total page weight down by 5.518KB. Given that the site receives about one million page views per day, the daily bandwidth savings could be 5.518GB. Over the course of a year, the site could save 2.014TB just by cleaning up a little markup! Let's assume that the site owners are paying a penny per gigabyte of traffic; that would be a savings of $16,112.

Building sites with web standards gives developers a chance to reduce data-transfer rates, lowering the cost of hosting. Building with standards makes pages leaner and faster, increasing the performance of the site and potentially lowering costs such as extra servers. By increasing the speed of page delivery and transactions, standards also help prevent the frustration that makes users quit web sites, vowing never to return. But improved performance and increased savings are not limited to the delivery of your site. The savings and performance benefits are just as substantial for site production and maintenance.

Part I: Lowering Production Costs

If your job were to build a new light bulb, would you create a new screw thread, or would you use the existing standard gauge? It is a silly question, really; one that would not even need to be asked of those of us living in a post–industrial-revolution world. We take standards for granted, and using the standard-gauge screw threads would be a matter of course.

But when it comes to making web pages, the value of working with standards is frequently overlooked. We web designers often waste time and money ignoring the economy offered by standards that exist in our own industry. We spend a shocking amount of time building bulbs for particular lamps, when we could devote those same (or fewer) resources to building bulbs that work on a wide variety of lamps.

The standards available are those defined by the World Wide Web Consortium, also known as the W3C (`www.w3.org/`). Simply put, W3C guidelines recommend how hypertext documents (web pages) should be marked up and how user agents— including browsers, PDAs, and Braille browsers—should display that markup.

Tipping our hat at the validation/markup wonks, we'll say that *web standards* is a term that covers so much territory that it has the potential to be vague. In general, it refers to the W3C's specifications and guidelines covering all aspects of markup, presentation, security, and encryption. In this chapter, we'll use *web standards* as web designers understand the term. Among knowledgeable web designers and developers, *web standards* colloquially refers to semantically meaningful markup, XHTML, combined with proper separation of that markup from the presentation using Cascading Style Sheets (CSS). The same is true for our use of the terms *standards compliant* and *standards-compliant pages*, used to describe this method of making sites.

By using the latest standards—XHTML for document structure and CSS for presentation—developers can create sites that work over time and across current and future browsers and other receiving devices, including assistive technology. Examples of assistive technology include screen readers that interpret browser content for the visually disabled, and alternative input devices that help people with limited mobility navigate web sites even though they are physically unable to use a mouse.

What Is the W3C?

The World Wide Web Consortium (W3C) is an international industry consortium. Founded in 1994 by Tim Berners-Lee, it now has more than 300 members. The hope is that the W3C's open specifications, which are colloquially called "web standards," will encourage interoperability: parts working together. Consortium members and invited experts form working groups that are charged with the task of writing these specifications. If accepted, the ideas are approved as formal W3C Recommendations.

The W3C has authored more than 40 Recommendations since 1994. HTML, XHTML, and CSS represent a small portion of that work. Other recommendations include these:

☐ Web Content Accessibility Guidelines 1.0: www.w3.org/TR/WAI-WEBCONTENT/

☐ HTML 4.0 Guidelines for Mobile Access: www.w3.org/TR/NOTE-html40-mobile/

☐ Extensible Markup Language (XML): www.w3.org/XML/

Members of the W3C include Sun, America Online, Microsoft, Apple, Ask Jeeves, Cannon, DoubleClick, and ERICSSON, among many others.

Definition: User Agent

For our purposes, a user agent is any virtual or hardware machine that can be used to access the Internet. Web browsers, PDAs such as the PalmPilot, Braille browsers, cellphones, and voice browsers are all examples of user agents that visitors might employ to access your web site. You will save time and money if you can stay user agent–agnostic as you build your site; plan for today's agents as well as tomorrow's.

If used properly, XHTML lends a rigorous structure to web sites, and CSS uses that structure to efficiently style those sites. The savings that you can enjoy in both producing a site and displaying it to a wide audience come from the fact that XHTML is doing the structural work and that CSS is doing the design or presentation work. This separation between document structure and presentation is the key. This is a separation that receiving devices, search engines, indexes, content-management systems, and other tools should be capable of taking advantage of.

Definition: Structure

When we speak of *structure* in web pages, we are talking about the semantic and hierarchic nature of markup. Meaning and logical hierarchy are what markup should really express. So, when you wrap a bunch of text in paragraph tags, you are assigning that text a place in the hierarchy of the document—namely, a paragraph. When you wrap a line of text in <h1> tags, you are assigning that line of text with the structural value of a header.

Definition: Presentation

When we speak of *presentation* in web pages, we are talking about how stuff looks in the browser. This is quite separate from structure, in that now we are defining how the paragraph and header elements look. The best, most efficient, and most economical way to handle presentation is to keep it separate from structure by letting HTML do the structural work and CSS do the presentation work.

If you work with web standards, you will enjoy two economic advantages:

1. You will spend less time and money on site development and even less time and money on site redesign.
2. You will have a product that works well on the greatest variety of receiving devices, including web browsers, PDAs, adaptive technology, and any newfangled device that might come along.

To realize these advantages, you need to follow three principles that are vital to the success of a shoestring web site:

1. As you build a site, try to separate document structure from document presentation.
2. Try to be as user agent–agnostic as you can be. (Don't design for one particular browser.)
3. Make a commitment to building well-made, durable sites.

> **Definition: Adaptive Technology**
>
> *Adaptive technology*, also known as assistive technology, is any hardware or software that makes a computer useable for people with disabilities. This broad category includes software that does such things as read text audibly, enlarge text, and make keyboards and other input devices easier to use for those with mobility impairments. It is difficult to tell from your web statistics whether users are accessing your site with adaptive technology; often a web browser such as Netscape or Internet Explorer is calling your site, but the user is viewing the browser with some form of adaptive tech. For more information on adaptive technology, see Joe Clark's book *Building Accessible Websites* (New Riders Publishing, 2002).

In the first part of this chapter, you learn how to do the important foundational work. In the second part, you enjoy the payoff by applying these ideas to a working web site.

> **Understanding HTML**
>
> This chapter assumes that you have at least some understanding of HTML. A good online resource is the W3Schools's HTML Tutorial (www.w3schools.com/html/). If you are looking for a book to cozy up with, consider Molly Holzschlag's *XML, HTML, XHTML Magic* (New Riders Publishing, 2001). I also recommend Jeffrey Zeldman's *Designing with Web Standards* (New Riders Publishing, 2003).

Good Markup: A Wise Investment

As many of us learned to build web sites in the 1990s, back in the days before the dreaded font and table elements were introduced, there was still a fair degree of semantics (structurally meaningful markup), but there were few ways to influence presentation in HTML. Your 1993 site could make structural sense, but you could not do much to make it look nice. When the `<font>` and `<table>` tags were introduced and browsers began to support them, designers ran wild, adding this new presentational markup to their pages.

This line of markup is what you had to write if you wanted a chunk of text to display in a smallish Arial font:

```
<font face=arial size=-1>Here is some text.</font>
```

For every chunk of text—whether a paragraph, a list, or a header—you had to write this junk.

Font tags were not the whole of this now-outdated method. In Chapter 6, "Content Management on a Tight Budget," I talked about the ubiquitous spacer GIF and recounted its tortured history as a makeshift margin producer. In the days of the 3.0 and 4.0 browsers, you had little choice; if you wanted padding, space, or margins, you cut a white or transparent image to the width or height that the whitespace required.

Web designers even had a good time creating designs that took advantage of problems of the early browsers. Back in the days of Netscape 1.0, if a developer wrote multiple `<title>` tags, Netscape 1.0 cycled through each, creating a slide show in the top chrome of the browser window. The following three `<title>` tags would have cycled through the title bar in an entertaining rhythm:

```
<title>Fancy Pants Magazine</title>

<title>A Weekly 'Zine for Fancy Pantzers</title>

<title>The Fanciest Pants in Town</title>
```

Playing with browser quirks and inconsistencies became an important skill; it was the designer's job to write markup that innovatively made use of the browser's flaws. The multiple `<title>` tag is a classic example that has passed into HTML history. The legacy of designing for specific browsers is strong, and most of the markup on the web draws upon these creative abuses.

This method of production, however creative, was a time-consuming endeavor, even if aided by graphical HTML editors such as Microsoft FrontPage and Macromedia Dreamweaver. However, this method was bulletproof. This markup would work in the few user agents designers had to worry about.

Presentational Markup Was Bad for the Web and for Web Developers

Although it was fun—and even though it allowed designers to control the way web sites looked—ultimately, presentational, browser-specific markup was bad for the web for four reasons:

1. Building sites was incredibly labor intensive, and redesigning them was often even more so.

2. HTML markup was not doing what it was supposed to do. Consider the `<title>` tag as an example. This element is supposed to tell user agents the title of a given page or site. If you had three `<title>` tags, which `<title>` tag was a search engine supposed to use?

3. Idiosyncratic HTML markup had to be remastered every time a new browser hit the market, making sites cost more.

4. Pages were bloated with extra markup, costing more time and money in storage and bandwidth consumption for designers and users.

Budget Threat

Bad, bloated markup will eat up your budget in several ways: by creating large HTML pages that are slow and expensive to serve, by making site maintenance and redesign a more protracted task, and by forcing you to create alternate versions of your site for nontraditional receiving devices. The responsible shoestring web professional saves time and money by authoring well-formed markup.

Many of us had to build sites this way; for some, the job was to make sites look good on a relatively small set of idiosyncratic web browsers. Production was intimately linked to what a site looked like on early versions of Netscape and Internet Explorer. With nearly every release of a new browser, it was necessary to go back to the sites and change that presentational markup so that it looked good in those new browsers. You could not afford to fall behind—and yet nobody could afford to keep up.

Good Markup Makes the Web a Better Place

But you do not have to do this anymore; in fact, you can't afford to. Browsers and markup have evolved, and you no longer have to spend time infusing markup with presentational garbage. Some 4.0 browsers began to move toward supporting markup more uniformly, but with the advent of Tasman (the rendering engine behind IE 5.0 for the Mac) and Gecko (the rendering engine behind Mozilla, post-4.*x* versions of Netscape, and several other browsers), different browsers began to interpret markup very similarly. The similarity is the result of the fact that browser manufacturers began to build user agents in accordance with W3C standards for (X)HTML and CSS.

At about the same time, designers began to recognize their responsibility for creating sites that work on other kinds of user agents, such as PDAs, Braille browsers, and cell phones. Fortunately, the W3C guidelines for mobile devices and web site accessibility mesh beautifully with XHTML and CSS, and sites built according to W3C standards work across user agents elegantly and predictably.

Your job today is quite different from that of a 1990s web designer: You must create well-crafted sites that work across a wide variety of receiving devices. The good news is that it is actually less work to do this. The approach should be to build one version of your site, and build it well, so that it works in all browsers and devices, old, new, and yet to come. In *Designing with Web Standards* (New Riders, 2003), Jeffrey Zeldman labels this new, cost-effective, standards-based approach to web design "forward compatibility," and his book shows how it works on both massive and more modest sites.

A Lesson in Separation of Structure and Presentation

The following figures and code illustrate the value of separating document structure from document presentation. Figure 7.1 and Listing 7.1 are the display and HTML of a site built the old-fashioned way. Figure 7.2 and Listing 7.2 are the display and HTML of a site built the new way. See how Spartan the markup in Listing 7.2 is compared to that in Listing 7.1? Listing 7.2 is lean and mean because it is free of all presentational markup.

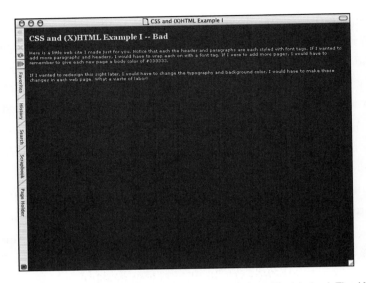

7.1 *Notice that the site was built with presentational markup. That is bad. The HTML is doing presentation work in Line 7 (highlighted in bold), where the body element has a color attribute. HTML is also doing presentational work in Line 8 (also highlighted in bold); inside the H1 tag, you see a long font tag that defines the color, size, and font face. A similar tag surrounds the paragraph elements that follow. This site's HTML is working too hard and utterly lacks economy.*

Listing 7.1 Markup for the Site Shown in Figure 7.1

```
<!DOCTYPE HTML PUBLIC "-//W3C//DTD HTML 4.01 Transitional//EN">
<html>
<head>
<title>CSS and (X)HTML Example I</title>
<meta http-equiv="Content-Type" content="text/html; charset=iso-8859-1">
</head>
<body bgcolor="#660066">
<h1>
<font color="#FFFFFF" size="+1" face="Georgia, Times New Roman, Times,
serif">CSS and (X)HTML Example I - Bad
</font>
</h1>
<p> <font color="#FFFFFF" size="-2" face="Verdana, Arial, Helvetica,
sans-serif"> Here is a little web site I made just for you. Notice that the
header and paragraphs are each styled with font tags. If I wanted to add more
paragraphs and headers, I would have to wrap each with a font tag. If I were
to add more pages, I would have to remember to give each new page a body
color of #333333.</font></p>
```

```
<p><font color="#FFFFFF" size="-2" face="Verdana, Arial, Helvetica,
sans-serif">If I wanted to redesign this sight later, I would have to change
the typography and background color, and I would have to make these changes
in each web page. What a waste of labor!</font></p>
</body>
</html>
```

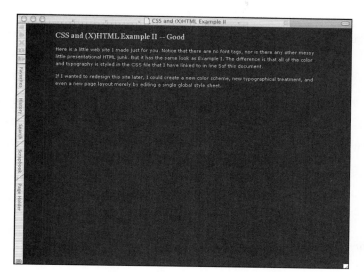

7.2 *This is nearly the same site shown in Figure 7.1, different only because it looks a bit better and because the HTML is doing only structural work, not presentational work. This is good. The job of presentation has been taken away from the HTML and given to the CSS document. The link that makes this happen is highlighted in bold in Listing 7.2. The reworked site looks better because the style sheet adds margins and leading to the paragraph.*

Listing 7.2   Markup for the Site Shown in Figure 7.2

```
<!DOCTYPE html PUBLIC "-//W3C//DTD XHTML 1.0 Strict//EN"
"http://www.w3.org/TR/xhtml1/DTD/xhtml1-strict.dtd">
<html xmlns="http://www.w3.org/1999/xhtml" xml:lang="en" lang="en">
<head>
<meta http-equiv="Content-Type" content="text/html; charset=iso-8859-1" />
<title>CSS and (X)HTML Example II</title>
<link rel="stylesheet" media="screen" type="text/css" href="styles/intro.css" />
</head>
<body>
```

continues

Listing 7.2 Markup for the Site Shown in Figure 7.2 Continued

```
<h1>CSS and (X)HTML Example II -- Good</h1>
<p>Here is a little web site I made just for you. Notice that there are no
font tags, nor is there any of the messy little presentational HTML junk. But
it has the same look as Example I. The difference is that all of the color
and typography is styled in the CSS file that I have linked to in Line 5 of
this document.</p>
<p>If I wanted to redesign this site later, I could create a new color
scheme, new typographical treatment, and even a new page layout merely by
editing a single global style sheet.</p>
</body>
</html>
```

In Listing 7.3, you see the style sheet that does the design work for Figure 7.2. This one style sheet can be used to style an entire site. If you need to make changes to the look of the site, you edit the one style sheet, and the look of the entire site follows suit.

Listing 7.3 Style Sheet for the Site Shown in Figure 7.2

```
1. body {
2.      color : #ffffff;
3.      background-color : #660066;
4.      margin-left: 70px;
5.      margin-right: 70px;}
6.  p    {
7.      font: 11px/18px verdana, geneva, arial, sans-serif;}
8. h1    {
9.      font: 18px/24px Georgia, Times New Roman, Times, serif;}
```

Let's look at all of the ways that this approach makes styling the little practice site immensely more efficient and less expensive to produce:

□ Instead of wrapping each paragraph element on the page in a long, cumbersome font tag, the rule on Line 7 of the style sheet in Listing 7.3 tells the browser that all paragraphs should be set in 11px Verdana. (If Verdana is not present on the user's system, then Geneva or Arial will be used; if these fonts are also unavailable, an alternative sans serif font will be pressed into service.)

□ All the pages on a site can link to one style sheet. Let's assume that the practice site comprises 40 HTML pages. The user downloads that style sheet only once; then the browser caches the style sheet. As the user downloads the remaining 39 HTML pages for the site, the style sheet has already been downloaded. You will save on bandwidth consumption (and so will your users).

□ If you need to make any changes to the look of the site, you just make a change to the style sheet. Let's say that you get a call from the client, who has decided that paragraphs set in Verdana make him ill; he wants all paragraphs to be set in Times New Roman or Georgia instead. With a standards-based design, you edit Line 9 of the style sheet, and the requested redesign is done. With old-school font tags, the changes might take hours of labor, depending on the number of pages the site contains and the variety of font tag stylizations used.

This practice style sheet is just a beginning; only three rules have been created—one for the body, a header, and a paragraph. You can build on this single CSS document to add more styles and variation. You learn how to add variety and complexity to your style sheet at the end of this chapter. You will see that the sky is the limit and that CSS offers not only a leaner site, but also more control over your layout than you could have ever hoped for with presentational HTML. Most important, you'll see how cheap your overall production costs become when you use CSS to control more of your site's presentation.

User Agent–Agnostic

As discussed in the previous chapter, about three years ago, my institution almost purchased a content-management system. One of the features that we were taken by with many CMS products was that the system could produce different pages for various receiving devices: one for each browser, one for Braille browsers and other forms of assistive technology, and other pages for handheld devices.

Now, the cost of producing various pages for different receiving devices or user agents is one that no one should take on. Don't ever let anyone convince you that you need to develop various versions of your site or that you need a tool that does that. Web standards can solve that problem *for free*.

Spinning Straw into Gold

By working with web standards, you are creating a site that works well in a wide variety of Internet devices, including traditional browsers, handheld devices, and assistive technology for people with disabilities. And you are serving all of these devices by creating only *one* simple version of your site. Web standards allow shoestring web professionals to do more with less.

By keeping presentational markup out of your XHTML document, and by keeping your XHTML markup clean, you keep your site user agent–agnostic. Text-based user agents such as some handheld devices, screen readers, and Braille browsers depend heavily on well-crafted markup and are unnecessarily burdened when they have to deal with the presentational junk.

In Figures 7.3–7.5, you see three views of The Web Standards Project (`www.webstandards.org`). Each screen capture is of the same site. Figure 7.3 shows the site in a traditional browser with style sheets turned on, Figure 7.4 is in a traditional browser with style sheets turned off, and Figure 7.5 is the site as seen in a PDA. One page works for all of these views. The site's navigation is just a bulleted list; the markup for that list is as about straightforward as XHTML can get.

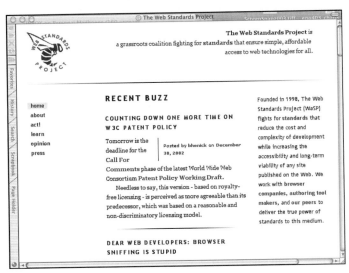

7.3 *The Web Standards Project is one of the forces that made standards support across web browsers what it is today (`www.webstandards.org`). This group has been working since 1998 to encourage browser manufacturers, software developers, and web authors to support web standards. This is one of the best sites to follow to stay on top of web standards news.*

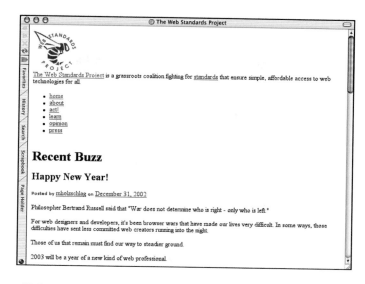

7.4 *You can see how the rigor of HTML stands up when the site is presented without style sheets...*

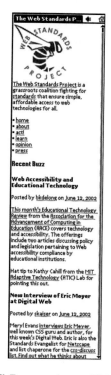

7.5 *...and on a PDA.*

The site would work equally well on a screen reader, a piece of software designed to read content on a computer screen to a visually impaired user. Like many other user agents, screen readers present content to the user based on the structure of the markup. A screen reader would read a bulleted list to the user with the proper emphasis and would pause between bullet points. Build once, display on many user agents. Make your site more accessible without spending a dime on needless multiple browser- and device-specific versions.

I have concentrated on using bulleted lists for navigation as an example, but this is just the tip of the iceberg. The second part of this chapter explores this "build once, use everywhere" idea in greater depth.

Web Site Accessibility Is Affordable

Did you notice how web site accessibility slipped into the last section as a matter of economic savings? Accessibility refers to the notion that a site should be as useable and accessible to people with visual, mobility, and other kinds of impairments as it is to any other user. An accessible web site is one that can be read by users on Braille browsers, voice browsers, and other such devices. As a bonus, it works just as well on web-enabled cell phones, PalmPilots, and other wireless and handheld gadgets. Accessibility is a topic that I care about deeply, but I bring it up indirectly and as a side dish for a reason. That is because when you build a site using web standards, accessibility becomes a matter of course, to a degree.

Well-crafted markup is the underpinning for building accessible web sites. If you create standards-compliant sites, you have automatically taken the first and most important step in creating an accessible site. Building sites this way is so easy that there really is no excuse for failing to make sites that are not at least minimally accessible, even if you are on a tight budget.

Clients and bosses are often reluctant to give the approval to build accessible sites. This is because many decision makers mistakenly believe that accessibility makes a site more expensive to produce.

It is your job as a web developer to know that by using well-understood standards and best practices, attaining a basic level of accessibility is not a matter of concern; it is a matter of course. Consider your boss's resistance a nonissue. By building with web standards, your sites will be at least minimally accessible, at no extra cost.

Think of the value you will bring to the stakeholders when they begin to worry about accessibility (if they are not worried now, they will be soon) and they find that your site is already on pretty solid ground. The vast savings that they'll enjoy by not having to redesign from scratch will be a feather in your cap.

If you need to learn more about making your web sites accessible—and you do—read Joe Clark's delightfully entertaining and remarkably comprehensive *Building Accessible Websites* (New Riders, 2002).

Build It Well

Aside from the accessibility and economic advantages of authoring well-constructed XHTML, it is also just plain cool to create something well made, a characteristic that is both practical and pleasurable. There was a phase in my life when I had time to find and fix up old furniture. If my Saturday morning at the flea market went especially well, I would come home with a beautifully made table or chair. As I fixed it up, my work was usually limited to cleaning and conditioning. If I came home with something that was not well made, I spent time covering up structural problems with glue, nails, and paint.

Building a site with well-constructed markup is like creating a well-made chair. Build it well, and it will bring pleasure for a long time. Even if you have to change the upholstery every few years to keep it looking fashionable, you will never have to mend it with glue and nails.

If pride is not a strong motivator, perhaps shame is. A few years ago, friends had a wooden deck built in the back of their new home. Expecting that the deck would add to the enjoyment and value of their home, they were saddened to see the deck fall apart after one year. The contractor had not used properly treated lumber to build it, and one year of rain, sun, and snow was enough to betray his bad work. My friends brought a small claims case against the contractor, who then had to take on legal fees.

It's difficult to predict what kind of liability we developers might be leaving ourselves open to when we build poorly constructed sites, but, as in any other industry, we have a responsibility to know and use the best practices in our field. Ignoring web standards makes us like the contractor who built a shoddy deck. It is, at the very least, bad form. End of soapbox.

The Mechanics of Good XHTML

Before you can enjoy the payoff of well-constructed XHTML, you must have a solid foundation in structured markup. If you are not already working this way, you will have to make a few simple mechanical adjustments and one more interesting mental adjustment.

It might take you some time to adapt to this new (although really very old) way of approaching markup. Do not be surprised by an initial slowdown in productivity. There is a learning curve every time you try something new, but this learning time will pay handsomely in the end. Sites will be easier to make and much easier to redesign. You will do much less with HTML; you'll write fewer lines of markup, and you will ask that markup to do less work. As a result, you will have pages that work well on the widest variety of browsers and other receiving devices.

You must do five simple mechanical things to write good markup:

1. **XHTML documents must begin with tags that tell the browser how to interpret them.** Begin your page with a Document Type Declaration (DTD) followed by an XHTML namespace declaration.

   ```
   <!DOCTYPE html PUBLIC "-//W3C//DTD XHTML 1.0 Transitional//EN"
   "http://www.w3.org/TR/xhtml1/DTD/xhtml1-transitional.dtd ">

   <html xmlns="http://www.w3.org/1999/xhtml" xml:lang="en" lang="en">
   ```

2. **Write all your tags in lowercase.** If you are in the habit of writing <H1>, <BODY>, and so on, kick the habit and write <h1> and <body>. Most HTML editors have a setting that enables you to write lowercase tags by default.

Definition: Document Type Declaration

A Document Type *Declaration* tells the browser which Document Type *Definition* (DTD) you are using. A Document Type Definition is a document that lists elements and attributes that can be used in an SGML, XML, or HTML document. A Document Type Definition describes where each tag is allowed and which tags can appear within other tags. Each version of XHTML has a Document Type Definition. Web developers can select from XHTML Transitional, XHTML Strict, and, when you want to partition the browser window into two or more frames, XHTML Frameset.

Definition: Namespaces

A *namespace* is a way to define or qualify the elements and attributes used in XML, HTML, or other marked-up documents. Because elements and attributes have the potential to become ambiguous across different DTDs and software, you must define the particular namespace that you are using. This might seem like a bit much at this point, but down the line, having this under control will keep your elements from being interpreted incorrectly by browsers and receiving devices. It is a lot to understand, but not a lot to do. Just be sure to include this line.

---

3. Quote all attributes. This is just a bit of housekeeping that is like keeping the cupboard doors closed. Back in the old days, you did not have to put quotation marks around width and height attributes. This was perfectly legal in HTML:

```
<img src="images/susan.gif" alt="Life can be good again." width=239
height=243>
```

XHTML requires that these attributes be wrapped in quotation marks, like this:

```
<img src="images/susan.gif" alt="Life can be good again." width="239"
height="243" />
```

4. Close all tags. This will be the most difficult change to adjust to. If you have formed bad habits, as most of us have, you will need a quantity of discipline. If you have an open <body> tag, you'll need to close it with a </body> tag. If you have an open paragraph tag <p>, close it with a </p>.

Here is the tricky thing about closing tags: You have to close even those tags that do not have an independent close tag. These buggers are called singleton elements because they are comprised of only one tag; they include meta tags, line breaks, and image tags.

Definition: Meta Tags

Meta tags in the header of a document describe the document. Meta tags exist for subject, author, keyword, and other descriptive elements about a page. Search engines and indexers use this data to describe and point to a site. Here are some meta tags taken from my personal site and correctly authored for XHTML with a closing space and slash:

```
<meta name="author" content="Carrie Bickner." />

<meta name="description" content="A web log about librarianship, web
standards and bibliographic delights.
Featuring reader-submitted library stories and photographs of New York
City." />

<meta name="keywords" content="Carrie Bickner, photographs, weblog,
gossip, style, libraries, accessibility, web standards, New York City." />
```

In the good old days of HTML 4.0 and earlier, a break tag looked like this:

```
<br>
```

In XHTML, it must close. Add a space and a slash to the tag:

```
<br />
```

An image tag in earlier versions of HTML looked like so:

```
<img src="shoe.gif" width="239" height="243"alt="Photograph of my most
recent shoe acquisition.">
```

In XHTML, you have to add the space and slash before you close the tag:

```
<img src="shoe.gif" width="239" height="243" alt="Photograph of my most
recent shoe acquisition." />
```

5. **Validate your pages.** At first it might seem intimidating, but you will soon find the validation process helpful, if not slightly addictive. Simply type the URL of the page on which you are working into the W3C's HTML validator (http://validator.w3.org/), as shown in Figure 7.6; then submit your markup and see just how good your XHTML is. This tool will catch most XHTML errors. As you learn to debug CSS, this tool will be your best friend.

Note

> If you find that the W3C validator is slow, try the Web Design Group's at
> www.htmlhelp.com/tools/validator/.

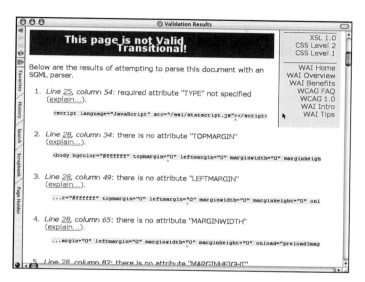

7.6 *The World Wide Web Consortium Validator is a tool that checks to see how correctly made (valid) your markup is. The validator gives you a line-by-line report of the errors in your markup. The first few times you use the validator, you will hate it; it feels like a difficult-to-read inventory of your personal shortcomings. But as you begin to fix the errors in your site, you will come to love this tool. It will become the friend whose honest answer keeps you from stepping out when you look bad.*

As you debug your first few pages, you will develop an understanding of markup that you probably have never had before. In the validator report in Figure 7.6, items 2, 3, and 4 point out that the body element of the page in question contains the deprecated attributes `topmargin`, `leftmargin`, `marginwidth`, and `marginheight`. Translated into English, this means that your body start tag contains four margin characteristics (attributes) that are not a part of the current XHTML specification.

Here is the bad markup:

```
<body bgcolor="#ffffff" topmargin="0" leftmargin="0" marginwidth="0"
marginheight="0" onload="preloadImages();">
```

Here is the good markup as you would rewrite it after reading the validator report:

```
<body onload="preloadImages();">
```

These particular body attributes are proprietary tags introduced by Microsoft and Netscape, and were never part of any formal W3C spec. Other validation errors catch elements and attributes that are now obsolete—that is, they were in a previous version of HTML but have now been kicked out of the club.

The good news is that invalid body tag attributes such as `marginwidth`, intended to control a presentational aspect of the site, are handled beautifully and much more economically by CSS. Rather than having to absorb the cost of including this markup on every single page, you can write a line on your style sheet that takes care of this formatting across your whole site.

Part II: The Payoff

Now that you have an idea of the principles of separating structure from presentation, it is time to build a site that uses them. The following examples help you jump in and show you the many layers of savings that come from building a site this way.

Step 1: Clean Up the Markup

As you can see in Figures 7.7 and 7.8, the same site has been implemented in different ways, with little change in the basic design. The site in Figure 7.7 has been executed the more expensive, old-fashioned way—the site uses HTML tables for layout, and color and typography are controlled with font tags and other presentational markup. Let's call this site Shoes Are Not Love—Bad.

Figure 7.8, Shoes Are Not Love—Good, is the same design executed with straightforward XHTML whose presentation is specified by a CSS style sheet. The markup for the outmoded version of Shoes Are Not Love comprises 104 lines of HTML markup and weighs 6.5KB. The spiffed-up version of Shoes Are Not Love is 62 lines of markup long and weighs 3KB. Let's make the site in Figure 7.7 into the site in Figure 7.8.

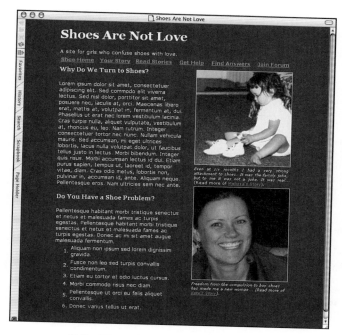

7.7 *Shoes Are Not Love—Bad.*

7.8 *Shoes Are Not Love—Good.*

Shoes Are Not Love—Bad has many of the common markup problems in today's poorly constructed sites. Let's clean them up one by one.

A Note About XHTML Document Types

Three flavors of XHTML 1.0 exist: Strict, Transitional, and Frameset. Many examples in this book use the strict DTD because it offers a greater separation of structure and presentation, and because it does a better job of anticipating future versions of XML and XHTML. By taking advantage of this separation and forward compatibility, you can find real savings. However, if you are stuck designing for Netscape 4.0, or if you are not ready to transition as quickly as this chapter urges, you might not be able to separate structure from presentation as aggressively as I have done. Netscape 4.0 has sketchy support of CSS, especially with respect to the layout work that CSS can do. If you are in this boat, you might need to rely on the more HTML 4.0-like flavor of XHTML, XHTML Transitional. You can also use tables to position at least some parts of your web page.

If you must use tables, try to use them as sparingly as possible. At any cost, avoid nesting tables inside tables for layout like this:

```
<table width="75%" border="1">
  <tr>
    <td>Some content positioned with a table. This is not a great idea.
      <table width="75%" border="1" align="left">
        <tr>
          <td>Some more content inside a table within a table. This is
          bad.</td>
        </tr>
      </table></td>
  </tr>
</table>
```

Netscape 4.0 browsers have good enough support of CSS margin and padding that you will not need to force that aspect of presentation with junk HTML.

The NYPL Online Style Guide (www.nypl.org/styleguide/) is a tutorial for how to take this exact approach. Jeffrey Zeldman and I created this guide for The New York Public Library because, like so many nonprofit and educational organizations, it was slow to move from Netscape 4.0 to a modern browser. If you need to take the softer, gentler way for now, use this guide to help you ease the transition to greater separation of structure from presentation. Zeldman's *Designing with Web Standards* shows in more detail how organizations can use this approach to achieve forward compatibility and accessibility while accommodating all users at a low cost.

Some CSS designs without tables work in Netscape 4.0, and these layouts enable you to stick with XHTML Strict and still please your Netscape 4.0 audience. You might want to do this rather than use XHTML Transitional. Soon enough, you will no longer have to worry about Netscape 4.0; when that time comes, you will want to have separated structure from presentation as much as possible so that all future redesigns will be easier on your resources. Craig Saila manages a list of CSS layouts that work in Netscape 4.0 (see www.saila.com/usage/layouts/nn4-layouts.shtml), and Mark Newhouse provides several such layouts for your use at www.realworldstyle.com.

Scrub the Head

The first thing to do is to clean up the HTML head. Listing 7.4 shows the outgoing, bad head, and Listing 7.5 shows the new and improved head.

Listing 7.4   Markup for the Header of the Site Shown in Figure 7.7

```html
<html>
<head>
<title>Shoes Are Not Love</title>
</head>
```

Listing 7.5   Markup for the Header of the Site Shown in Figure 7.8

```html
<!DOCTYPE html PUBLIC "-//W3C//DTD XHTML 1.0 Strict//EN"
➥"http://www.w3.org/TR/xhtml1/DTD/xhtml1-strict.dtd">
<html xmlns="http://www.w3.org/1999/xhtml" xml:lang="en" lang="en">
<head>
<meta http-equiv="Content-Type" content="text/html; charset=iso-8859-1" />
<title>Shoes Are Not Love</title>
<link rel="stylesheet" media="screen" title="2 Column - left hand navigation"
➥type="text/css" href="/styles/basic.css" />
<style type="text/css" media="all">@import "/styles/fancy.css";</style>
</head>
```

Notice that the following have been added:

- The XHTML Document Type Declaration in Line 1 and the XML namespace in Line 2 (see Listing 7.5).

- A meta tag that tells the user agent what character set it has to work with. The fact that the markup in Listing 7.5 is longer than the markup in Listing 7.4 might be a bit counterintuitive at first. After all, web standards are supposed to reduce bandwidth consumption, not increase it with additional tags and attributes. Generally, cleaned-up markup is much, much shorter than old-school stuff, but the addition of Document Type Declarations and the like make the header longer.

- The title tag for the site. This is also shown in Figure 7.7, and theoretically even old-school web designers know to always include the title tag. But if I had a nickel for every web page without a title that I have seen, I would not be writing a book about tight budgets. The title tag helps search engines and directories find and appropriately index your site's content. Use it or lose potential visitors.

> **Definition: Character Set**
>
> A character set is a defined list of characters or symbols recognized by hardware and software. Each character is represented by a number. Many character sets exist, so for web pages to be understood by browsers and other receiving devices, a character set needs to be declared.

□ A link to two style sheets. You can call them whatever you want—here they're called basic.css and fancy.css. What is important is how you call those two style sheets. Line 6 calls a style sheet with the `link` method, and Line 7 calls a style sheet with the `import` method.

Here is why you are going to love this: I mentioned earlier that Netscape 4.0 has sketchy support of style sheets. It is so sketchy, in fact, that some parts of CSS will cause Netscape 4.0 to choke. However, Netscape 4.0 does not understand the `import` method for calling style sheets. So, when you add something to your site that Netscape 4 would be better off without, add that style to the CSS document that is called with the `import` method.

□ Closure for the `<head>` element.

Scrub the Body

Now that there's a nice clean head, you can move into the body of the document. Some tools will help you do this. HTML Tidy is a fine one (see `http://tidy.sourceforge.net/`). Dreamweaver MX also has validation and cleanup tools that are invoked if you use an XHTML Document Type Declaration (see `www.macromedia.com/software/dreamweaver/`).

Listing 7.6 shows the Shoes Are Not Love site styled with font tags. Notice how bulky the font tags make the page.

Listing 7.6 Markup for the Body of the Site Shown in Figure 7.7

```
1.  <h1><FONT COLOR=#FFFFFF SIZE=3 face=Georgia, Times New Roman, Times,
2.  serif>WHY DO WE TURN TO SHOES?</FONT></h1>
3.      <P><FONT COLOR=#FFFFFF SIZE=-1 face=Verdana, Arial, Helvetica, sans-
4.  serif> Lorem ipsum dolor sit amet, consectetuer adipiscing elit. Sed
5.  commodo elit viverra lectus. Sed nisl dolor, porttitor sit amet, posuere
6.  nec, iaculis at, orci. <a href="erat.html"> Maecenas libero erat</A>,
7.  mattis at, volutpat in, fermentum at, dui. Phasellus ut erat nec lorem
8.  vestibulum lacinia. Cras turpis nulla, aliquet vulputate, vestibulum at,
9.  rhoncus eu, leo. Nam rutrum. Integer consectetuer tortor nec nunc. Nullam
10. vehicula mauris. Sed accumsan, mi eget ultrices lobortis, lacus nulla
11. volutpat dolor, ut faucibus tellus justo in lectus. Morbi bibendum.
12. Integer quis risus. Morbi accumsan lectus id dui.
13. <a href="sapien.html">etiam purus sapien</a>, tempus ut, laoreet id,
14. tempor vitae, diam. cras odio metus, lobortis non, pulvinar in, accumsan
15. id, ante. aliquam neque. pellentesque eros. nam ultricies sem nec
16. ante.</FONT>
17.     <h2><FONT COLOR=#FFFFFF SIZE=3 face=Georgia, Times New Roman,
18. Times, serif>DO YOU HAVE A SHOE PROBLEM?</FONT></h2>
```

Listing 7.7 is nearly the same site, but this version is styled with CSS. The link to the CSS is just one line in the header of the document (not shown), so the rest of the markup can be left to do only structural work. Notice how lean this chunk of markup is.

Listing 7.7 Markup for the Body of the Site Shown in Figure 7.8

```
1.  <h2>Why Do We Turn to Shoes?</h2>
2.  <p>Lorem ipsum dolor sit amet, consectetuer adipiscing elit. Sed commodo
3.  elit viverra lectus. Sed nisl dolor, porttitor sit amet, posuere nec,
4.  iaculis at, orci. <a href="erat.html">Maecenas libero erat</a>, mattis at,
5.  volutpat in, fermentumat, dui. Phasellus ut erat nec lorem vestibulum
6.  lacinia. Cras turpis nulla, aliquet vulputate, vestibulum at, rhoncus eu,
7.  leo. Nam rutrum. Integer consectetuer tortor nec nunc. Nullam vehicula
8.  mauris. Sed accumsan, mi eget ultrices lobortis, lacus nulla volutpat
9.  dolor, ut faucibus tellus justo in lectus. Morbi bibendum. Integer quis
10. risus. Morbi accumsan lectus id dui. <a href="sapien.html">Etiam purus
11. sapien</a>, tempus ut, laoreet id, tempor vitae, diam. Cras odio metus,
12. lobortis non, pulvinar in, accumsan id, ante. Aliquam neque. Pellentesque
13. eros. Nam ultricies sem necante.</p>
14. <h2>Do You Have a Shoe Problem?</h2>
```

Scrubbing up your HTML is easy, and it becomes even easier as you practice. Four simple steps are involved:

1. **Make sure that all XHTML tags are in lowercase.** You can set your HTML editor to write lowercase markup by default. Even if you do not move from HTML to XHTML right away, you should start to write markup in lowercase so that you are in the habit and so that your pages make the transition more easily when the time comes. Listing 7.6 shows a mix of uppercase and lowercase tags; that is bad. In Listing 7.7, all tags are in lowercase; that is good.

2. **Quote all attributes.** Most of the attributes in Listing 7.6 will go away when you remove the presentational markup from the site; you'll be rid of font and size attributes. Other attributes, such as the `href` attribute to the link element in Listing 7.6, need the quotation marks that you see in Listing 7.7.

3. **Close all elements.** The proper way to talk about this is in terms of "start" and "end," so let's be proper. Listing 7.6 has a paragraph start tag in Line 3 that should close in Line 16 but that does not. For shame! Listing 7.7 ends with the analogous end paragraph tag on Line 13.

4. **Remove presentational markup from your HTML.** You already know that you need to do things such as remove presentational attributes like those shown next from the body tag:

```
<body bgcolor="#333333" text="#FFFFFF" link="#6699FF" vlink="#6699FF">
```

All that's needed is a simple body tag, like this:

```
<body>
```

You also know that you have to strip font tags such as those in the first four lines and the last three lines of Listing 7.6.

Removing this junk is just the beginning of ridding your site of presentational markup. You might also want to kill the HTML tables.

Tables Cost Too Much

One of the biggest wastes of bandwidth and labor is HTML tables. The old version of Shoes Are Not Love (see Listing 7.8) uses several tables to control layout. Some, such as the photo sidebar, are nested inside other HTML tables. Although you had to build sites this way in the days of primitive browsers, it is a good idea to avoid this technique now.

This chapter has harped on the idea of separating structure from presentation; using tables keeps these two pieces yoked. Structurally, HTML tables are for data. They are meant to hold information such as lists of employee names and phone numbers, or grids of products and costs.

Listing 7.8   Markup for the Navigation Shown in Figure 7.7

```
<tr>
<td width=16%><div align=center><strong><font size=-1 face=verdana, arial,
➥helvetica, sans-serif><a href=two.html>Shoe Home</a></font></strong>
➥</div></td>
<td width=16%><div align=center><strong><font size=-1 face=verdana, arial,
➥helvetica, sans-serif><a href=index.html>Your Story</a></font></strong>
➥</div></td>
<td width=17%><div align=center><strong><font size=-1 face=verdana, arial,
➥helvetica, sans-serif><a href=two.html>Read Stories</a></font></strong>
➥</div></td>
<td width=15%><div align=center><strong><font size=-1 face=verdana, arial,
➥helvetica, sans-serif><a href=onea.html>Get Help</a></font></strong>
➥</div></td>
<td width=18%><div align=center><strong><font size=-1 face=verdana, arial,
➥helvetica, sans-serif><a href=two.html>Find Answers</a></font></strong>
➥</div></td>
<td width=18%><div align=center><strong><font size=-1 face=verdana, arial,
➥helvetica, sans-serif><a href=three.html>Join Forum</a></font></strong>
➥</div></td>
</tr>
```

Even more important to those on limited budgets is the fact that tables are ridiculously labor intensive to build and redesign. Assume that you wanted to alter the site navigation in Figure 7.7 by changing "Your Story" to "Share Your Story." With each menu item in its own table cell, you would need to adjust the width of each table cell that holds the menu items. If you wanted to add another photograph and caption to the sidebar, you would again have to edit tables. Each photo and caption in the sidebar is in a separate table cell, so if you wanted to add more photos and captions to the sidebar, you would need to create more table cells. If you are trying to save time and money, get yourself out of the table business.

In Figure 7.8, the top navigation has been taken out of a table and given a meaningful structure: an HTML list (see Listing 7.9). If you wanted to change "Your Story" to "Share Your Story," you would just edit that list item.

Listing 7.9   Markup for the Navigation Shown in Figure 7.8

```
<div id="menu">
<ul>
<li><a href="index.html">Shoe Home</a></li>
<li><a href="/story/">Your Story</a></li>
<li><a href="/read/">Read Stories</a></li>
<li><a href="/help/">Get Help</a></li>
<li><a href="/answers/">Find Answers</a></li>
<li><a href="/forum/">Join Forum</a></li>
</ul>
</div>
```

Scrubbed Up and Ready to Go

When you have finished cleaning your site, you should have a page that looks just like Figure 7.9. This is just a plain vanilla HTML page. When you have removed the junk and produced a simple, well-structured (X)HTML document, you can begin to take advantage of the economy and power of Cascading Style Sheets.

7.9   *Before you create the style sheet, the site should look like a plain old HTML site. In fact, one way of making sure that you have done a good job of marking up a site is to view it without style sheets. If the content flows well, take this as an indication that you have a page with solid semantic markup. You'll have a good idea of the intellectual presentation that users of nongraphical browsers such as PDAs and Braille browsers will receive.*

Making Style Sheets

Now let's build a style sheet that gives Shoes Are Not Love—Good the same layout as in Shoes Are Not Love—Bad. In Chapter 5, "The Design: Looking Good with Less," you started a table that you used to organize the way you wanted to treat typography (see Table 5.1). You can use that table as basis for creating your style sheet.

Style sheets are made up of rules, and rules are made up of selectors, values, and properties. This whole chunk of text is a CSS rule:

```
body {
    color: #ffffff;
    background-color: #333333;
    margin-left: 70px;
    margin-right: 70px;}
```

The browser knows that the rule is to be applied to the body of an HTML page because of the first line, the body selector. Following the body selector is a curly bracket, which tells the browser that it is about to receive some properties. The first property is color; this is the font foreground color. The value of that property is #ffffff, the hexadecimal value for white. A shorthand version, #fff, might be used instead to save a few bytes of user bandwidth. This is pretty simple stuff. Make sure that you use the colon to separate the properties from their values. Some people mistakenly use the equals sign, which is intuitive but incorrect.

Following the color property are a few more properties and their values. Notice that a semicolon separates each style property from its brothers. The final style property in a rule need not end in a semicolon, but it is a good idea to use it anyway, to add consistency and to avoid errors if you later change the order in which properties are listed or add additional properties. There's a background property with a value of #333333, a nice dark gray, and right and left margin properties that each have the value of 70px. The closing curly bracket indicates that the rule has been defined. So now there's a CSS document with one rule that creates a site with white text, a dark gray background color, and left and right margins of 70px.

You can add to it by creating more rules and by adding more properties and values to those rules. Now that you know what to call each of the parts of a CSS document, you can build one for the Shoes Are Not Love site.

Let's create a style sheet that gives the same design that Figure 7.8 has, except that the new design will take advantage of some of the power that only CSS provides. We'll begin with the simple stuff: color and typography.

Color and Typography

You are looking for a dark gray background, white text, and two different type-faces: Verdana for the copy and Georgia for the headings (see Listing 7.10). Of course, as discussed in Chapter 6, if this were a working style sheet, you would have fallback typefaces to ensure that the design works on a variety of platforms, including those that don't offer Verdana or Georgia. So include those fallback faces in the style sheet.

Listing 7.10   Cascading Style Sheet for the Site Pictured in Figure 7.8

```
 1. body {
 2.        color: #ffffff;
 3.        background-color: #333333;
 4.        font-family: verdana, geneva, arial, sans-serif;
 5.        margin-left: 70px;
 6.        margin-right: 70px;}
 7.
 8. div, p, th, td, li, dd, dl, dt {
 9.        color : #ffffff;
10.        font: 11px/18px verdana, geneva, arial, sans-serif;}
11.
12. h1, h2, h3, h4, h5, h6    {
13.   color : #ffffff;
14.   font-family: georgia, times new roman, times, serif;
15.   margin-bottom: 1px;}
16.
17.   h1    {
18.        font-size:    1.8em;
19.        text-transform: uppercase;
20.        text-align: justify;}
```

Lines 1–18 of the basic.css style sheet (see Listing 7.10) take care of these typographical and color jobs for the entire site (see Figure 7.8).

Line 1 begins the rule for the body selector. Line 2 gives the color property the value of #ffffff, or white. Line 3 defines the site's background color (#333333, or dark gray), and Line 4 defines the default typeface as Verdana, Geneva, Arial, or whatever sans serif font the user has on the machine.

Lines 5 and 6 add a bit more to the body rule and, in doing so, take on a job that tables previously had to do: They define the margin that appears on the left and right sides of the content. Just two lines of CSS to do a job that scores of HTML tables used to do. This, sirs and ladies, is economy.

CSS is not entirely economical, however, at least in the way that it is supported across browsers. CSS is supposed to offer economy by allowing children to inherit properties from their parents. A paragraph rule, for example, should inherit its properties and values from the body rule. The style sheet should not have to be redundant. But inheritance is tricky across browsers, especially for Netscape 4.0. That's why there's a long-winded rule in Line 8. This rule is for divisions, paragraphs, table headers, table cells, and a variety of list items. You have to make it explicit to some browsers that each of these elements must display in white, so Lines 9 and 10 define color, font, and font size for a whole slew of elements. Still, this is much more efficient than wrapping every line of text in a font tag.

Lines 12–15 define the rule for a mess of header elements. These properties and values tell browsers that headers should display in white Georgia (or Times New Roman or Times, depending on the fonts on the user's system).

Values and properties are all it takes. You can add whatever values and properties you like. Many of these values and properties do things that plain old HTML just can't do because it was never intended to do them. A few of these are described next.

Margins, Leading, and Other Empty Spaces

You might have noticed that in Line 10, font size is expressed as 11px/18px, and Line 15 defines the bottom margin for all headers as 1px. Here CSS is doing some finesse work that simply can't be done with presentational HTML. 11px/18px tells the browser to render text at 11px, but to give a pinch of whitespace (leading) between lines. If you go back and compare Figure 7.7 (old school, no leading) to Figure 7.8, you will see how leading improves the readability of the copy in the latter example. Similarly, the 1px margin under the header elements allows text to snuggle gently up against the header above. This makes it easier to visually identify a paragraph as relating to the header just above it. Old-school HTML formatting cannot do this.

For more information about margin, padding, and leading, see the Cascading Style Sheets 1 specification on the W3C's site (www.w3.org/TR/REC-CSS1). It is much to wade through, but it is well worth it. A List Apart offers easy-to-read CSS tutorials (www.alistapart.com/stories/indexCSS.html).

Transforming Text

Let's have just a bit more fun before moving from typography to page layout. You can easily transform text with CSS. Line 17 has a rule that defines the h1 element with more care (see Listing 7.10). Line 19 contains a text-transform property with the value of uppercase. This tells the web browser to transform the text in all <h1> elements to uppercase. You can use text transform to do things such as change the first few words of a paragraph to uppercase. Again, the Cascading Style Sheets 1 specification on the W3C's site will tell you how to use text transform—see www.w3.org/TR/REC-CSS1.

Page Layout

Now that typography and color have been put to bed, let's make a layout for the site. The layout is a simple one. To create it, you need to break the page into three conceptual chunks: the navigation, the sidebar, and the main copy area. Then you need to create rules that present these intellectual chunks in distinct areas of the screen.

When you cleaned up the HTML page, you turned the navigation into a bulleted list. Now you get to play with CSS to control the display of this list. You could create a rule for all unordered lists, but that would make all unordered lists look like navigation. And your site will probably contain some plain old unordered lists that have nothing to do with navigation. So you need to create a special rule that applies only to the unordered list in the navigation area. You do this by creating an *identifier* that enables the style sheet to create a special look just for the list in the navigation.

CSS Class Selectors and ID Selectors

CSS makes use of class selectors and ID selectors to pick out and style certain blocks of HTML from a web page. They work almost the same way, but identifiers are to be used only once on a page, while classes can be used repeatedly. Use class selectors when you want to style an element that will appear multiple times in a page, such as a paragraph or a header. Use an ID selector when you want to have a unique element in a page, such as a navigation bar or a headline.

ID selectors are created in a style sheet with a pound sign (#). The syntax looks like this:

```
#someidentifier {
}
```

This is called out in the HTML document with any element that has an id attribute, like this:

```
<div id="someidentifier"></div>
```

Class selectors look just the same, but instead of using the pound sign, they use a dot:

```
.someclass {
}
```

They are picked out in the HTML document with a class attribute, not an id attribute:

```
<div class="someclass"></div>
```

Selectors can and should be used across a site. When you create names for them, try to make them as meaningful and as easy to remember as you can. If you have top and side navigation, use selectors such as topnav and sidenav. A colleague of mine took to giving selectors cute but meaningless selector names, such as pumpkinbox. If I had a penny for every time I had to go back to the style sheet to remember the name of that selector, I'd be spending my weekends at Saks instead of Macy's. When you redesign, you will be grateful to have appropriately named selectors in your style sheet and markup; the fact that they are logical and easy to remember will make the redesign job easier.

Note that this is just the beginning of the story: There are also type selectors and universal selectors. Detailed rules govern how each of selectors can be used. To brush up on these before you get in too deep, see www.w3.org/TR/1999/REC-html401-19991224/types.html#type-id.

On the XHTML page, you need to attach the identifier (or id) to the navigation list. Listing 7.11 shows the unordered list wrapped inside a division, or div, tag.

Listing 7.11   Simple Markup Reduces the Bulk of the Site

```
14. <div id="menu">
15. <ul>
16.    <li><a href="index.html">Shoe Home</a></li>
17.    <li><a href="/story/">Your Story</a></li>
18.    <li><a href="/read/">Read Stories</a></li>
19.    <li><a href="/help/">Get Help</a></li>
20.    <li><a href="/answers/">Find Answers</a></li>
21.    <li><a href="/forum/">Join Forum</a></li>
22. </ul>
23. </div>
24.
25. <div id="sidebar">
26. <p><img src="images/carrie1_6mo_c.gif" alt="Shoe addiction can take even
the young." width="239" height="243" />
27. <cite>Even at six months i had a very strong attachment to shoes. It was
the family joke,
28. but to me it was not a joke. It was real...</cite> (read more of <a
href="story.html">Melissa's
29. story</a>).</p>
30. <p><img src="images/susan.gif" alt="life can be good again." width="239"
height="243" />
31. <cite>Freedom from the compulsion to buy shoes has made me a new
woman...</cite> (read more of
32.    <a href="story.html">Kate's story</a>).</p>
33. </div>
34. <h2>Why do we turn to shoes?</h2>
35. <p>Lorem ipsum dolor sit amet, consectetuer adipiscing elit. Sed commodo
elit viverra lectus. Sed nisl dolor, porttitor
36. sit amet, posuere nec, iaculis at, orci. <a href="erat.thml">maecenas
libero erat</a>, mattis at, volutpat in,
37. fermentumat, dui. Phasellus ut erat nec lorem vestibulum lacinia. Cras
turpis nulla, aliquet vulputate, vestibulum at,
38. rhoncus eu, leo. Nam rutrum. Integer consectetuer tortor nec nunc. Nullam
vehicula  mauris. Sed accumsan, mi eget
39. ultrices lobortis, lacus nulla volutpat dolor, ut faucibus tellus justo
in lectus.
40. Morbi bibendum. Integer quis risus.nmorbi accumsan lectus id dui. <a
href="sapien.html">etiam purus sapien</a>, tempus ut, laoreet id, tempor
vitae, diam.
41. Cras odio metus, lobortis non, pulvinar in, accumsan id, ante. Aliquam
neque. Pellentesque eros. Nam ultricies sem nec
```

```
42. ante.</p>
43.
44. <h2>Do you have a shoe problem?</h2>
45. <p> Pellentesque habitant morbi tristique senectus et netus et malesuada
fames
46. ac turpis egestas. Pellentesque habitant morbi tristique senectus et
netus
47. et malesuada fames ac turpis egestas.</p>
```

The div tag has the id of menu. That's all you need. You could have given that id any name, but it is best to give it a name that makes sense and that is easy to remember and easy to spell. Now the CSS rules that you create for that identifier will be applied to that division.

So, let's make that rule—or, in this case, rules. You'll need to have three CSS rules to pull off this look. Listing 7.12 shows how that job is done. The example continues the CSS document we started in Listing 7.10, where we styled the basic page elements such as the body, paragraphs, and headers.

Listing 7.12   A Style Sheet Will Do the Presentation Work

```
21. .first      {
22.      margin-top: 0;
23.      padding-top: 0;
24.      text-transform: uppercase;}
25.
26. #menu ul, #menu li {
27.      display: inline;
28.      margin: 0;
29.      padding: 0;
30.      color: #333399;
31.      text-transform: uppercase;
32.      text-align: justify;}
33.
34. #menu ul {
35.    width: 800px;}
36.
37. #menu li a {
38.    padding: 7px;
39.    background: #666666;
```

continues

Listing 7.12 A Style Sheet Will Do the Presentation Work (Continued)

```
40.     color: #ffffff;
41.     border: solid 1px #999999;
42.     text-decoration: none;}
43.
44. #menu li a:hover {
45.     background: #333333;}
46.
47. #sidebar {
48.     width: 245px;
49.     text-align: justify;
50.     padding: 20px, 0px, 20px, 20px;
51.     float: right;}
```

The rule that begins in Line 26 sets the general characteristics of the unordered list. This rule defines the look of the text and establishes that the list will run horizontally instead of as the traditional vertical list display:

- Line 27 includes a display property with the value of `inline`. This tells the browser that you want the unordered lists and list items with the `menu id` list to display inline (horizontally, not vertically). Note that this does not guarantee that the text won't wrap; it ensures only that the browser will not force a line break after each list item.

- Line 32 contains a `text-align` property with a value of `justify`, as opposed to a left or right alignment.

- Line 37 begins a rule that defines how each linked list item will display. This is where you make the cute little rollover buttons. You do not need to use JavaScript to create rollovers; text and CSS can do it for you. This is how you can create the rollover off state: On and off states refer to the position of the mouse relative to the object on the page. When the mouse or cursor is placed above the object, this is an on state. When the cursor or mouse is moved away from the object, that is an off state.

- Line 38 gives the menu items a dose of padding so the text can breathe.

- Line 39 gives the menu buttons a light gray background.

- Line 40 makes the text white.

- Line 41 gives each button a 1px border.

To create the rollover on state, Lines 44 and 45 tell the browser that when the user rolls over the link, the background color of the menu button should change to dark gray (#33333).

Now for the sidebar. All you want to do with the sidebar is to make it display on the right side of the browser. Again, create a special id, this time called sidebar. Attach that id to the chunk of the page that you want to appear in the sidebar (see Listing 7.11, Line 25). Then create an id in the style sheet that you see in Line 47 of Listing 7.12. The CSS rules for the sidebar say to make this area 245px wide, justify the text, give it a smidge of padding, and float it to the right of the page.

As you create more styles for your site, make sure that you preview them in a wide variety of browsers. If you run into a style that makes Netscape 4.0 unhappy, just remove that style from your basic.css document and put it in the fancy.css style sheet. Netscape 4 is not the only browser that will hiccup on a CSS rule, but it is the least CSS-compliant of browsers currently in use. Moving Netscape 4-unfriendly rules to the imported fancy.css style sheet protects Netscape 4 from its failings and gives people who use that browser a better experience.

Quick and Easy Redesign

Let's say that the Shoes Are Not Love client decides at the last minute that she *hates* the design. She signed off on the first design, true, but remember that she is recovering from a major shoe problem and is probably unstable. You look to the client for a paycheck, not for consistency. Now she wants the site to be pink, and to have a pretty background pattern with lots of little bees flying around because bees mean power, or so she believes. She wants some fancy typefaces, and she wants the sidebar to be on the left. You just want this client out of your life. Because you used CSS to implement the design, you can resolve this quickly.

7.10 *Shoes are Not Love redesigned in a snap.*

You spend the better part of 30 minutes editing your style sheet and, against every aesthetic principle you ever stood for, produce the site in Figure 7.10. This is what you had to do:

- Add a background image property to the body rule; this involved writing one more line in the CSS document. Note that no image was added to the body tag in your HTML page.

```
body {
        background-image: url(images/bees.gif);}
```

- Shift the location of the sidebar from right to left by changing yet another single line in the style sheet: The sidebar rule's `float` property was changed from right to left:

```
#sidebar {
        width: 245px;
        text-align: justify;
        padding: 20px 0px 20px 20px;
        float: left;}
```

- Fiddle with a few more CSS rules by changing a few more properties and values. Change some typefaces, sizes, and margins by adjusting a handful of CSS properties and values.
- Bill the client for the extra 30 minutes. She deserves it.

Creating a Print Style Sheet

A simple print style sheet can control how your page prints. You can use this style sheet to hide navigation and other page elements that might just waste paper. You can also select typefaces that are more suitable for print. Listing 7.13 shows a style sheet that prints the Shoes Are Not Love site in the style that you see in Figure 7.11.

7.11 *If you want some control over how your page looks when printed, you can quickly create a style sheet exclusively for the printer.*

Listing 7.13   New Printer Style Sheet for Shoes Are Not Love

```
body {
      color: #000;
      background-color: #fff;
      font-family: verdana, geneva, arial, sans-serif;
      margin-left: 70px;
      margin-right: 70px;}
div, p, th, td, li, dd, dl, dt {
      color : #ffffff;
      font: 11pt verdana, geneva, arial, sans-serif;}

h1, h2, h3, h4, h5, h6   {
      font-family: Georgia, Times New Roman, Times, serif;
      margin-bottom: 1px;}

h1   {
      font-size:   24pt;
      text-transform: uppercase;
      text-align: justify;}
h2   {
      font-size:   20pt;}
h3   {
      font-size:   18pt;}
h4   {
      font-size:   14pt;}
h5   {
      font-size:   .12pt;}
h6   {
      font-size:   11pt;}

a {
color: #99cccc;
text-decoration: underline;
font-weight: bold;}
a:hover {
text-decoration: none;}
a:active {
color: #99ffff;}
```

```
img {
border: dotted 1px #cccccc;}

.first    {
     margin-top: 0;
     padding-top: 0;
     text-transform: uppercase;}

#menu ul, #menu li {
     display: none;}

#sidebar {
     width: 245px;
     text-align: justify;
     padding: 20px, 0px, 20px, 20px;
     float: right;}
```

Listing 7.13 shows a style sheet that will format the document for printing. It is based on the style sheet that was redesigned for the crazy client, but with a few important changes that are designed to make the content look good on paper:

- Body text font sizes are no longer expressed in pixels and ems, which are the best ways to designate font size on the web; they're expressed in a point size. Point sizes are intended to be used in print.
- Everything that is wrapped in the menu id (`#menu`) above is hidden. The clever `display: none` rule takes care of this. Why waste paper a printing a nav bar?
- All background colors are gone; only the white background for the body rule remains. Users will be cross if you waste their toner printing background colors that do not translate well to print. (And some browsers don't print background colors anyway.)

When the user prints the site, he will see a page formatted like the document in Figure 7.11.

XHTML and CSS Resources

In this chapter, I've barely hinted at the power of CSS. If you have well-crafted XHTML markup, you can do many things with CSS. Here are a few resources that you can turn to when you want to learn more:

- The idea of creating an inline list like the one in the Shoes Are Not Love site navigation came from an A List Apart article called "Taming Lists," by Mark Newhouse (`www.alistapart.com/stories/taminglists/`).

- As mentioned earlier in the chapter, Mark also manages a site called Real World Style (`http://realworldstyle.com/`). He likes to create layout problems and find CSS solutions for them. The solutions are often beautiful, and many of them work acceptably even in Netscape 4.

- The Web Standards Project (`www.webstandards.org`) is a fine place to stay on top of news, tutorials, and, if you feel so moved, community action in nearly every aspect of web standards.

- Eric Meyer has created many fantastic resources, including a few books on the topic: *Eric Meyer on CSS* (New Riders Publishing, 2002), *Cascading Style Sheets: The Definitive Guide* (O'Reilly & Associates, 2000), and *Cascading Style Sheets 2.0 Programmer's Reference* (The McGraw-Hill Companies, 2001). He also maintains a list of resources on his site, Meyerweb (`www.meyerweb.com/eric/css/`).

- Jeffrey Zeldman is my personal favorite web standards evangelist. Zeldman's *A List Apart: A Magazine for People Who Make Web Sites* (`www.alistapart.com`) regularly features articles on the mechanics of creating standards-compliant web sites. His Daily Report follows standards-related news (`www.zeldman.com`), and his book *Designing with Web Standards* fills in where this chapter leaves off. I know that because as I write this book, he is sitting behind me writing his book. We don't get out much.

Chapter 8

Bang-for-Your-Buck Hosting and Domains

Chapter Checklist

1. **Buyer, beware.**

   Although there are many well-run domain name registries and hosting companies, others probably belong to SPECTRE. Protect your pocketbook from the sharks by staying organized and doing your research.

2. **Watch out for hidden costs.**

   Hidden costs such as site downtime and difficult-to-reach support lines can eat up a site's budget quickly.

3. **Beware of bandwidth blues.**

   Many hosts will slap you with bandwidth charges if your site traffic increases. Make sure that you know what your bandwidth limits are and how much you will pay if you go over that limit. Keep an eye on your site's statistics; if your traffic is increasing, that is a good thing, but you should not pay a winner's penalty fee. It is your responsibility to know what your transfer rates are and to know how much bandwidth costs. You will save money if you stay on top of the information.

4. **Do it yourself.**

   Remember that you can host your own site. If you like to roll up your sleeves and get under the hood, the do-it-yourself option could provide the best bang for your buck.

" *Groucho: It's all right—that's in every contract. That's what they call a "sanity clause."*
Chico: Ha. ha, ha, ha. ha! You can't fool me—there ain't no Sanity Claus. "

—Groucho and Chico Marx in *A Night at the Opera* (1935)

In 2002, as I began to build and manage a small, professional web site for a friend, I registered her domain name with easyDNS (www.easydns.com), a reliable domain name registrar. A month or two later, I received a "domain name expiration notice" from another registrar; let's call them StinkyDomains. The notice from StinkyDomains was a form to "renew" the domain that I had just registered with easyDNS. The document was designed to imply that I had reserved the domain with StinkyDomains, not easyDNS, and to suggest that the domain was about to expire. As I studied the form, I saw that the apparent expiration date was actually a thinly veiled "reply by" date and that the accompanying form was not a renewal, but a transfer authorization. Had I fallen prey to this trickery, I would have moved the domain to StinkyDomains and would have been needlessly charged an extra $35 for a year of domain registration.

These crude tactics are unethical and might even be illegal (or borderline illegal), but they go on all the time. Many a designer or site owner has paid needless fees to companies in response to deceptive "expiration notices." Nobody should be suckered this way, and no shoestring designer can afford it.

My troubles have not been limited to domain names; hosting, too, has been a source of pain. In 1999, I opened a web hosting account with a hosting company that we'll call NastyHost. The first two months were a joy, but in the third month, my site started to come and go; it was down for days at a time. So I canceled the service, found a new host, and moved on with my life. Or so I thought.

A year later, I opened a credit card statement and found that NastyHost had charged my account $1,141.20 out of the blue. After a bit of research, I discovered that they claimed to have no record of my cancellation and that they had assumed that I wanted to continue the long-dead site, but on a new, more expensive plan. The particular hosting plan that I had purchased years ago was no longer available, so they had thoughtfully selected a "similar" plan that cost four times as much and saved me the trouble of deciding how to spend my own money by billing my credit card directly. To make matters worse, these hosts notified the domain registrar of my "new" location, and the registrar believed them. The record was updated to point to a server I wasn't using. People trying to visit my site could not do so. Straightening out this mess and securing the refund was a 10-day affair; I was on hold for a total of 6 hours.

Sadly, a web professional's position on hosting and domain names is too often a defensive one, and much of my advice to the shoestring professional is along the lines of maintaining a strong defense against these kinds of problems. In this chapter, I'll help you make sure that you can protect yourself. Don't fret: This chapter is not all doom and gloom. We'll find good value hosting and domain name services.

Definition: Domain Name Registration

A *domain name* is an alphanumeric name that enables you to define hosts—usually, but not always, single computers—within that domain. Hostnames enable users to refer to the easily remembered name (such as www.example.com) instead of a hard-to-remember IP address (such as 66.45.6.196), which is how browsers and web servers actually communicate. ebay.com is a domain name, in which is defined a hostname, www, which points to the server that provides the site: www.ebay.com. A domain name *registrar* is a service that enables you to register a domain name and then define a hostname in that domain to point to the place on the Internet that your site will call home.

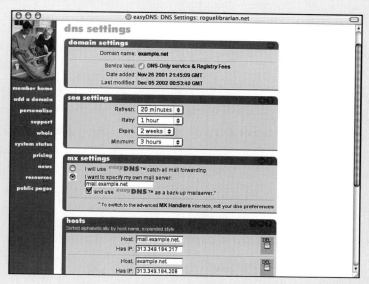

When you register a domain name, you create a record like the one you see here: www.easydns.com. In the last section of the record, under Hosts, you can see that the domain name, www.example.net, is pointing to a host IP address. In this case, the made-up IP address 313.349.184.208 is the host machine, and the domain name registrar will have www.example.net point to that IP address.

> **Definition: Web Hosting**
>
> A web-hosting service provides the server space where the files that make up a site reside. A server is just a computer that runs software that *serves* your pages to those who view them. If your site is large, these computers must be powerful, must run almost all the time, and must be joined to the Internet with a fast connection. For a smaller-scale site, a server can be relatively underpowered; if your site doesn't eat a lot of bandwidth, it doesn't even need a fast connection (but it still must run almost all the time).

Buyer Beware

I wish I could say my tragicomic domain and hosting experiences described earlier were an exception to the rule, but that is not the case. And it's not just me: Every web professional I know has run into domain and hosting snafus that would shock the Better Business Bureau. The prudent shoestring web professional keeps an eye out for charging practices, site downtime, and bad technical and customer support, and, above all else, stays organized.

Remember that time is money. Returning to my six-hour telephone experience with NastyHost, if we were to figure that a client or boss had been paying me about $20 per hour, my experience with NastyHost cost $120. This does not take into account potential loss of revenue one might experience when a site is unavailable for days. Remember, NastyHost not only charged me big bucks for a server I wasn't using, but it also prevented visitors from seeing my site. If you experience this kind of forced downtime or slog through these time-consuming support issues, it is costing you big bucks. When you are on a shoestring budget, this loss is difficult or impossible to absorb.

Here is the good news: There are well-run, honest domain registration and hosting companies, and there are things that you can do—in fact, *must* do—to protect yourself from the bad ones. If you are smart about hosting and domains, your budget just might stay in the black. Let's walk through domain name registration and hosting, and explore the things you can do to save money and to protect yourself from unanticipated expenses.

Your Domain Name Dollar

Domain name registration is not something to try to *save* money on. The goal at this stage of the game is to keep from *wasting* time and money. Do this by avoiding deals that seem to good to be true and by keeping good records.

If It Sounds Too Good to Be True...

At the time of publication, registering a domain name for a year costs around $35. If a registrar offers the service for $12, be suspicious—you might face hidden costs later, or you might be charged "per-usage" fees each time you update your address or other information in your account.

It Pays to Be Organized

It is imperative that you keep good records. You need to know with whom you registered your domain, when you did it, how much you paid, and which credit card you used.

The predatory practices that nearly got me in trouble with StinkyDomains are terribly widespread. Simply do a Google search on "domain name scams" to see what the latest swindle is. On the Internet, the rights of corporations are pretty well protected: Try using an image you don't own or streaming a music file you haven't paid for, and you'll quickly find yourself on the losing end of a court case. Alas, the rights of ordinary consumers, freelancers, and web professionals are not as well protected. Imagine that you are in the Wild West; even if you are not looking for trouble, you need to carry a gun and know how to use it simply to survive.

Good records make excellent ammunition. You must keep careful records in your own office, of course, but you must also keep your contact information current with your domain name registrar. Even well-intended registrars can't help you if you change addresses without telling anyone. If you do not keep contact information up-to-date with your domain registrar, you will not receive renewal notices.

You have to keep your own records in good shape as well. If you have multiple domains, and most web professionals do, it is hard to keep these records in your head. If you have one file, you can determine quickly which forms you receive in the mail are legit and which are not. In addition to keeping a file of all your transactions, keep a spreadsheet like you see in Table 8.1. You need to be able to tell at a glance where your domain names are registered. File it under penny-wisdom.

Table 8.1   Worksheet for Keeping Track of Your Domain Names

Domain Name	Registrar	Registration Date	Expiration Date	Cost	Credit Card Number	Username and Password	Reseller (Y/N)	Notes
Wishiwasher.com	SPECTRE DNS	June 30, 2001	June 29, 2002	$150	6543 XXXX XXXX XX352	U: bornyesterday P: p0wd3rpuff	Yes	Why did I trust them? They lost my account, so now I can't renew. Have to register .net and .org so people can at least find my site again.
Wishiwasher.net	UFP DNS	May 22, 2002	May 22, 2003	$35	4567 XXXX XXXX XX309	U: notthistime P: ssm00chk1tt3n	No	So far, so good.
Wishiwasher.org	UFP DNS	May 22, 2002	May 22, 2003	$35	4567 XXXX XXXX XX309	U: notthistime P: d1rtys0ck3	No	Support guy sounds cute. Dare I send him secret URL of private photos?

If you get funny-looking email messages or form letters regarding your domain, look them over carefully before you send off checks or credit card numbers. Examine your credit card statements every month to make sure that you are not being charged for services you never ordered.

Decision: Selecting a Domain Name Registrar

As discussed earlier, a domain name registrar is a service that enables you to "buy" a domain and point it to a server. *Buy* is a misleading word because you're really *registering* the domain, and only for a limited period of time. One-, two-, and five-year registrations are the most common, and there is usually a price break if you pay for more than one year in advance. When you have a host set up, you use the registrar to configure a hostname in your domain to point to a server.

The oldest and best-known registrar is Network Solutions (Netsol). This ancient registrar is now owned by VeriSign (www.verisign.com), but most web pros still call the company Network Solutions, along with some less flattering names. It would be an understatement to say that serious customer service issues have plagued Netsol and its customers since the day the service launched. An entire site is dedicated to these issues (www.nsihorrorstories.com). Reading them will curdle your blood like last month's milk. Some, no doubt are apocryphal.

In fairness to Netsol, the bigger you are, the more customers you have, and thus the more customer complaints are likely to crop up. Still, given the number of stories of sketchy customer support that hang on this company, there might be better places to spend that $35. Also, although Netsol is far and away the biggest and most successful registrar, it is not above sending deceptive "renewal" notices to people who've registered with competitors.

easyDNS (www.easydns.com) is a smaller domain name registrar. The cost of registration is the same, but as this book goes to press, the customer support is still excellent and the overall value of this service remains high.

With prices as low as $8.95, Go Daddy (http://meet-the-makers.com/conversations/parsons/) is another alternative, and despite its low prices, its level of customer satisfaction is high.

easyDNS and Go Daddy are not the only good games in town. For a definitive list of registrars, see Internic's *The Accredited Registrar Directory* (www.icann.org/registrars/accredited-list.html). ICANN is the only body that can accredit a registrar in the .com/.net/.org top-level domains.

Note

The Frugal Host

Securing a domain name is all well and good, but it is not much without a web host to point to. Like domain name registration, web hosting can be a hornets' nest of hidden costs ready to sting the unwary shoestring developer right in the softest part of her budget. When selecting a host, shoestring professionals should do the same kind of evaluation and planning work we did in Chapter 6, "Content Management on a Tight Budget," as we looked for the best content-management system for the bucks:

1. Know what you want.
2. Know which hosts can give it to you.
3. Take the time to learn how these services work.

Know What You Want

After reading the preceding chapters, it will come as no surprise to learn that I love to shop. There is only one reason that I have not shopped myself into poverty. Before I head out on a spree, I determine my budget and create a mental inventory of what I have. Then I make a list of what new pieces will help me get the most of what I already have. Do the same thing when you shop for a web-hosting provider.

Rather than inventorying your closet, take a look at what you have—traffic reports, number of employees, size of your site—and then consider the following issues:

1. What is your annual or monthly budget for hosting? Bear in mind that this includes labor costs in terms of the time you'll spend dealing with technical support.
2. Will your site receive bags of traffic? If so, you will need considerable bandwidth and a high transfer limit (I'll show you how this works later). Check the statistical reports on your existing site. If you do not have these numbers, try to find out how many bytes similar sites transfer.
3. Will you need to have a database-driven site? What kind of database and middleware software will you need? Many sites are driven by content that resides in databases such as MySQL, Oracle, or Microsoft SQL Server that is then delivered to the web page by a piece of middleware such as PHP, ColdFusion, or ASP. Open-source options such as MySQL and PHP are less expensive than their commercial counterparts, including MS SQL Server and ColdFusion. But if you are already developing with a commercial product, the transition could cost too much in terms of production.

Budget Threat

Many hosting services offer Microsoft Access as their "web database" program. Although the ubiquity of Access makes it a tempting, inexpensive solution for database-driven sites, the program is not well suited to the web; it can't hold up to much traffic and was never intended to do this job. If you skimp on your database, you will pay later in site performance. See Chapter 6 for more about the Access problem and for tips on low-cost, database-driven sites.

4. If your site will be database-driven, check to see how well the potential host manages database applications on shared servers. Some hosts cram too many inept ColdFusion programmers onto one box; talk about a prescription for costly downtime. One site I worked on went down repeatedly as a third-party site owner on the same server taught himself ColdFusion programming. A good host monitors and corrects these kinds of problems.

5. Will you need to have many mailboxes, as you might on a corporate or organizational site? Will the mailboxes require much disk space on the server? If you will need oodles of email storage, make sure that your hosting plan accommodates that need. Otherwise, you could run into over-limit charges (or even lost and nondelivered messages). Remember, too, that a web-based email client keeps mail on the server unless you manually delete your messages. A mail client such as Eudora or Outlook Express can and should be set to delete messages from the server as they are downloaded. Setting that preference correctly can help you avoid over-limit charges and professionally embarrassing blocked in-boxes (where customers write to you and their messages bounce because your mailbox is full).

6. Assume that your demands on support will be high, and make good technical and customer support a top priority. If you are on a budget, you can't afford to spend much time on hold. A smaller local hosting company might better serve you than an automated giant located who knows where. Even though the big company might charge slightly less per month, your time is worth money, and your site's uptime is priceless.

7. Assume that monkeys staff your potential host's tech support, and be ready to test them. Think of a technical question that you know the answer to. See how they answer. If you turn to your host's systems people for advice and support, be sure to get a second opinion from someone not connected to the hosting company. The host's people might be ill informed. In some cases, they might even provide misleading answers simply to avoid doing work you've requested. Find a host whose technicians know what they're talking about, and then double-check what they tell you against your own research.

8. Assume that you need to have things such as a web site statistics package so that you can keep an eye on your site's traffic. You might need this information if the bandwidth dragon ever rears its ugly head. Also ask if the host provides access to raw logs—some people want more detailed information than the host's default statistics package provides. You might want to crunch this data on your own.

9. Know what kind of management access you desire. If you like to get under the hood, make sure you have FTP and shell access. If you want just a graphical interface, see if you can administer your site with your web browser. You don't want to discover that you have the wrong interface after you have given your host your credit card number.

10. Ask if you can get a money-back guarantee. It is worth a shot.

The Cost of Bandwidth and Disk Space

Let's work with a real-world example to get a handle on the cost of bandwidth and disk space. iwebhosting.com is quite explicit about how it charges for bandwidth (see Figure 8.1). Make sure that you have this information up front and that you understand what it means. Let's use this basic plan as an exercise: $10 a month gives you 25MB of disk space and 1000MB of monthly transfer. If you go over either of these limits, you are charged about a tenth of a U.S. penny per megabyte.

Disk space is relatively cheap; this is the amount of storage you have on the server. Bandwidth, on the other hand, is not so cheap; this is the amount of data that your site transfers in a given period of time. You will be charged for exceeding either disk space or bandwidth rates. Know what the charges are, in case you exceed them. Also ask how the provider keeps track, how it notifies you, whether it restricts you to a set disk/bandwidth allocation, whether it charges you after the fact, and so on.

Let's see how disk space and bandwidth charges work, and how choosing the right plan can make all the difference to a shoestring site.

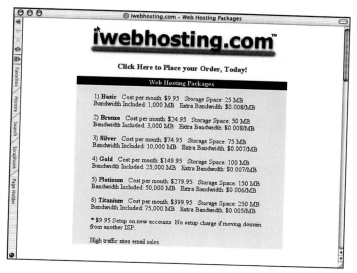

8.1 *iwebhosting's bandwidth charges (*www.iwebhosting.com*).*

iwebhosting's web-hosting packages are pretty straightforward: As storage and transfer rates increase, the packages go up. Notice that each package also includes a fee for extra bandwidth. That is the amount that you will be charged if you go over the monthly bandwidth allowed. Let's examine how various packages would serve the following two sites simply in terms of bandwidth (see Figures 8.2 and 8.3). You will see that it pays to give careful attention to your bandwidth consumption and to stick with hosting packages that most closely match your needs.

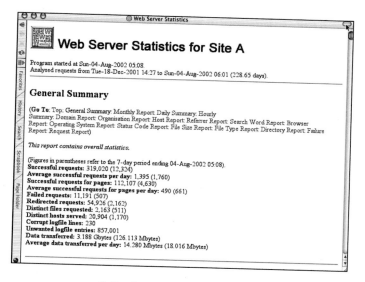

8.2 *Bandwidth use for Site A.*

The bandwidth use for Site A is expressed in two ways in the second-to-last line of the report listed as Data Transferred. The first number, 3.188GB, is *total* transfer for the time since statistics have been kept (228 days). The second number, 126.113MB, is for the past week. The more reliable indicator is the 3.188GB in 228 days figure, which amounts to 97MB per week, on average. But the fact that the last week was 28MB *more* than the average weekly consumption for the past 228 days suggests that the site is getting more popular or is getting heavier. Either way, more bandwidth is being used, and this can be indicative of a possible trend.

iwebhosting's basic plan would be suitable, assuming that the average transfer rate continues, but if the site begins to transfer more than 1000MB per month, as it seems poised to do, the owner will be charged $0.008 for each megabyte over that 1000.

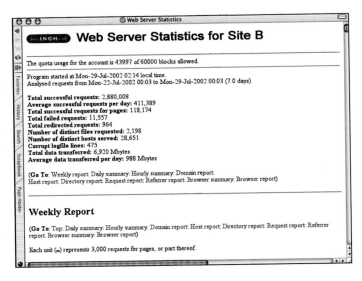

8.3 *Bandwidth use for Site B.*

The report for Site B also shows how much data was transferred in a week; in this case, it is 6920MB of data transferred in seven days. 6920MB × 4 is 27,680MB; that is (roughly) how much data is transferred in one month. If Site B were on iwebhosting's Bronze plan, the data-transfer limits would have been surpassed by 24,680MB. At an extra bandwidth charge of $0.008 per megabyte, extra bandwidth would have cost

$197.44 in addition to the monthly base charge of $24.95. The total for that month's hosting activity would have been $222.39 instead of the expected $24.95. It is important to keep an eye on your bandwidth use and switch to a more appropriate hosting plan as your data transfer increases. In this case, Site B would have had a less expensive month if it had started with the iwebhosting's Gold plan; $149.95 would have covered all of that activity.

Spinning Straw into Gold

To lower your bandwidth cost, try to keep your site lean. You can keep your pages trim by writing well-formed markup, as we discussed in Chapter 7, "Save Time and Money with Web Standards." Pages that are marked up well tend to be smaller and thus less expensive to serve. Consider the cautionary tale in the first paragraphs of Chapter 7 about a well-known, heavily used e-commerce web site that needlessly wastes about a terabyte of bandwidth transfers per year on bloated markup.

It is your responsibility to keep an eye on your account; if your site grows in size or popularity, you are the one who will need to ask the hosting company about upgrading your package. As soon as the numbers indicate that your site is about to outgrow its existing plan, move immediately to a higher tier. By switching to a more expensive monthly plan that allows higher data-transfer amounts, you could save much money over a cheaper plan with lower data-transfer allowances.

Know, too, that some hosts don't care how much traffic you get: They charge only by the amount of disk space you use. If you can find a good host that charges only for disk space, go with it. Site B resides on a commercial host that charges only for disk space. Site B's owner pays about $50 a month, which is a lot better than $222.39.

Measure Twice: Bits and Bytes

Bit

Bit stands for binary digit and is the smallest unit of information on a computer. When we speak of 0s and 1s, we are talking about bits. A single bit can hold only one of two values: 0 or 1. A bit is abbreviated as a "b."

Byte

Byte stands for binary term, which is a unit of storage that holds a single character. A byte is equal to 8 bits. I have a silly but helpful pneumonic for remembering the difference between bits and bytes. A byte is meaningful; you can take a bite out of it. A byte is abbreviated as a "B."

Kilobyte

Normally, a kilo stands for 1,000, but because computers are binary, or Base 2, a kilo is 2 to the 10th power. So, 1KB is technically 1024 bytes. *Kilobytes* are usually expressed as K or KB.

Megabyte

A *megabyte* is 2 to the 20th power, or 1024KB.

Gigabyte

A *gigabyte* is 2 to the 30th power, or 1024MB. When you talk to hosting companies, pay careful attention to those who talk in terms of charging by the gigabyte and those who charge by the giga*bit*. A byte is 8 bits, so the math can be quite different. Don't be surprised when a sales rep fails to recognize that a stats report in megabytes or gigabytes is not the same as one in megabits or gigabits. Network engineers usually speak in bits; salespeople selling disk space speak in bytes.

Do the Math

Barbie was right: Math is hard. But do it anyway. Make sure you know what you're getting charged for, what is meant by "kilo" or "mega," and whether a 1,024 multiplier or a 1,000 multiplier is used. However inaccurate they might be, some people use the term *kilobyte* to refer to 1000 bytes rather than the correct 1024 bytes. The vague-minded might use the term *megabyte* to refer to 1000KB when they more accurately should use that term to refer to 1024KB. The difference between 1,000 and 1,024 can add up over a year of hosting activity.

Also bear in mind that you can't simply measure transfer in terms of a multiple of the size of the pages you've served. There is always overhead used by the act of transferring data. When large files are transferred, they must be broken up into smaller packets, and each packet will incur what you might think of as "shipping costs."

Imagine that you had ordered a 12-piece set of porcelain dishes. The weight of the set might be 24 lbs., but the set must be broken into 12 separate boxes. For each box, you might need to pay for the box, foam, and tape. What's true for dishes is true for data: As a large file is sent along, each packet requires routers to keep track of it. These costs might be negligible in each individual instance, but they add up over time. It would be overkill to worry about the fractions of cents that these "packet shipments" cost, but the fiscally responsible web professional always has these expenses in the back of her mind.

Finding the Price Is Right Host

Now that you know what you want, it is time find a host that can give it to you. Word of mouth is a terrific starting point; talk to happy site owners and look into their hosts. It is still important to do the due diligence work yourself. You need to know the details of the plan that you buy and keep an eye open for Groucho's sanity clause.

A place to start cold research is Web Host Ratings (www.webhostratings.com). This site is an independent guide to web hosting. Its database of hosts includes user reviews, plan descriptions with detailed overviews of features, and costs for hundreds of hosting companies.

One interesting report that this site provides is a hosting company's downtime, which Web Host Ratings checks on a regular basis. This is nice to see, but if Web Host Ratings checks only from one place on the network, it could be unfairly penalizing a host for network problems that reside upstream. Just because I can't get to a site when I'm connected to the Net via a dialup ISP doesn't mean that the site is down. More often, the dialup ISP is having upstream connectivity problems. The site could be fine.

The user reviews at Web Host Ratings are illuminating (see Figure 8.4). I did a few searches on the hosting company that sent me the bill for $1,141.20, and I discovered that I was not alone. I found scores of reviews that complained not only about unauthorized credit card charges, but also locked domain names, unreachable tech support, Rip Van Winkle–length periods of site downtime, and other expensive problems. Keep in mind that user reviews tend to contain the views of a self-selected group; you have to ask how that group was selected. Did they all share a bad experience, or did they all forget to pay their bills? I felt vindicated by the stories that I found and am inclined to believe that there are serious issues with that hosting company. Of course, all of us would do well to remember that there are two sides to every story.

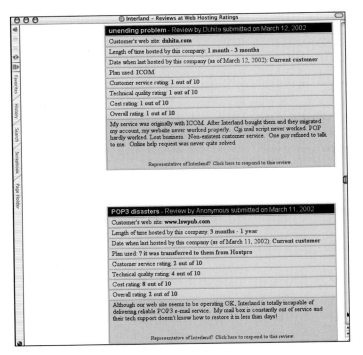

8.4 *Web Host Ratings (www.webhostingratings.com) is an independent guide to hosting companies. Reader-submitted comments and objective statistics will help you zero in on a few appropriate plans.*

As you conduct your research, you might make a chart like Table 8.2. Put your needs in the top row, and begin filling in the cells as you conduct your research. Pay careful attention to extra costs such as setup fees and over–limit charges as you work.

Table 8.2 Worksheet for Comparing Hosting Companies

Plan	Monthly Cost	Server OS	Disk Space	Transfer Limit	Server Features	Data-bases	Set-Up Fee	Mail-boxes	Uptime Guarantee	Money-Back Guarantee	Tech Support	Word of Mouth
Fancy Pants Hosting	$16	Windows 2000	200MB	10GB Extra transfer cost: $1 per gigabyte	Perl, PHP, ASP	MS Access	$15	Unlimited	99.996%	30 days	M–F, 9–5 EST	Bad reviews on Web Host Ratings.
Smarty Pants Hosting	$30	Linux	Unlimited	20GB Extra transfer cost: $20 per gigabyte	Perl, PHP	MySQL	None	35	Will not say.		No	Email only Have not found any.
Dirty Pants Hosting	$10	UNIX	50MB	Unlimited	Perl, PHP	MySQL	None	10	99%	No	24×7	Catherine uses them.
Hot Pants Hosting	$30	UNIX or Windows 2000	100MB	Unlimited	CFM, ASP	None	Not sure	Unlimited	99.999%, but reviews suggest this is not the case.	90 days	24×7	There is an entire site dedicated to how much this host sucks.

A Note About Uptime

When a host lists any information about uptime, whether it is a guarantee or a history, do the math. A site that is up 99.9% of the time will be down for about a third of a day over the course of an entire year. Most sites will be brought down half a dozen times for an hour or two at a time to move servers, perform upgrades, and handle routine maintenance when necessary. This is normal and is generally planned in advance by a hosting company. Your host should let you know when your site will be down, and will most often schedule it when business is not at its peak. It's not hard to get a 99.99999% uptime figure; that's down two days in five years.

Gather a good range of hosts that are within your budget, and try to select the one that does the best job of matching your listed needs. *Do not let the lowest price be the only thing that drives your decision.* Saving $5 or $10 a month will mean nothing if your host fails you. Remember that a shoestring budget does not mean that it is time to go bargain basement shopping.

Just Give Me a Cheap Host

Research is well and fine, but you might need to jump straight into a list of cheap hosts. Remember, however, that if it sounds too good to be true, it probably is. Some companies disappear without warning because they made the mistake of trying to offer cheap service that never quite made them the profit necessary to stay in business. Perhaps the most important quality in a host is whether a company will be around tomorrow.

Remember also that new hosting companies sometimes offer low prices to build up business. As their operations grow, hosts can:

- Raise their rates and change the terms of your contract without telling you.
- Slap you with bandwidth charges.
- Cram hundreds of sites onto your shared server, killing the speed of your site and leaving it vulnerable to crashes and downtime.
- Fail to make enough money to stay in business, and then disappear silently.
- Be bought by someone else, who raises your rates and possibly lowers your service.

All of that you-get-what-you-pay-for said, here is a list of places to check for cheap sites:

- ❑ **Web Host Ratings List of Cheap Hosts**
  (`www.webhostingratings.com/cheap.html`)—This list of five top cheap hosting plans is updated regularly and is based on a variety of data, including user feedback.

- ❑ **Free Web Hosting Solutions on About.com**
  (`http://html.about.com/cs/freewebhosting/`)—Jennifer Kyrnin has been the host of the XML/HTML section of About.com for years. Although About.com itself is a faded rose, Jennifer's work remains quite good. Her list of free web hosts is up-to-date and well researched.

- ❑ **Spoke and Axle Free Web Hosting**
  (`http://spoke-and-axle.com/`)—If your site is noncommercial, check Kelly Abbott's Spoke and Axle's "dating service" (see Figure 8.5). This site matches those in need of hosting with those who are willing and able to host. Spoke and Axle is Abbott's response to the bandwidth robbery suffered by the likes of Al Sacui of Nosepilot.

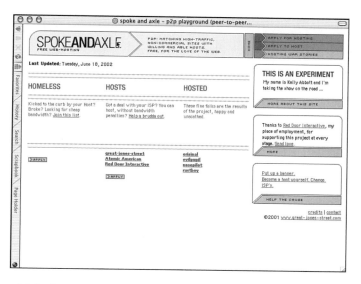

8.5 *Spoke and Axle (`http://spoke-and-axle.com/`) is a site created by Kelly Abbott that is dedicated to matching the bandwidth-poor with the bandwidth-rich. Free hosting might be something people will offer for an art site such as Nosepilot or because they are sympathetic to a site's particular cause. Do not expect this generosity to be extended to a for-profit business.*

As a design or content professional, you might never have intended to learn about web hosting, and you might not relish the thought of comparison shopping unless it is for your George Foreman Grill. But taking on unanticipated tasks is part of the game for shoestring web designers—and doing those tasks well can make all the difference between failure and success.

All design is a challenge, and shoestring design is a challenge on top of a challenge. But shoestring design also presents us with a priceless opportunity to learn every aspect of our craft.

Shoestring design challenges us to do more with less. It prompts us to push our skills harder (while continually learning new ones) and to truly focus on what our users need and what our sites absolutely, positively must deliver.

Shoestring design is not for the rich and famous, although shoestring designers have occasionally spun straw into gold and low-budget sites into fame and fortune. It is also not for the unmotivated or the easily discouraged. But if you keep at it, you will grow creatively and professionally in ways you never imagined. And that is something no amount of money can buy. See you in the discount rack!

Index

www.informit.com

YOUR GUIDE TO IT REFERENCE

New Riders has partnered with **InformIT.com** to bring technical information to your desktop. Drawing from New Riders authors and reviewers to provide additional information on topics of interest to you, **InformIT.com** provides free, in-depth information you won't find anywhere else.

Articles

Keep your edge with thousands of free articles, in-depth features, interviews, and IT reference recommendations— all written by experts you know and trust.

Online Books

Answers in an instant from **InformIT Online Books'** 600+ fully searchable online books.

POWERED BY

Safari

Catalog

Review online sample chapters, author biographies, and customer rankings and choose exactly the right book from a selection of over 5,000 titles.

New Riders

www.newriders.com